ZENTANGLE

Adult Coloring Book

H L Gailey

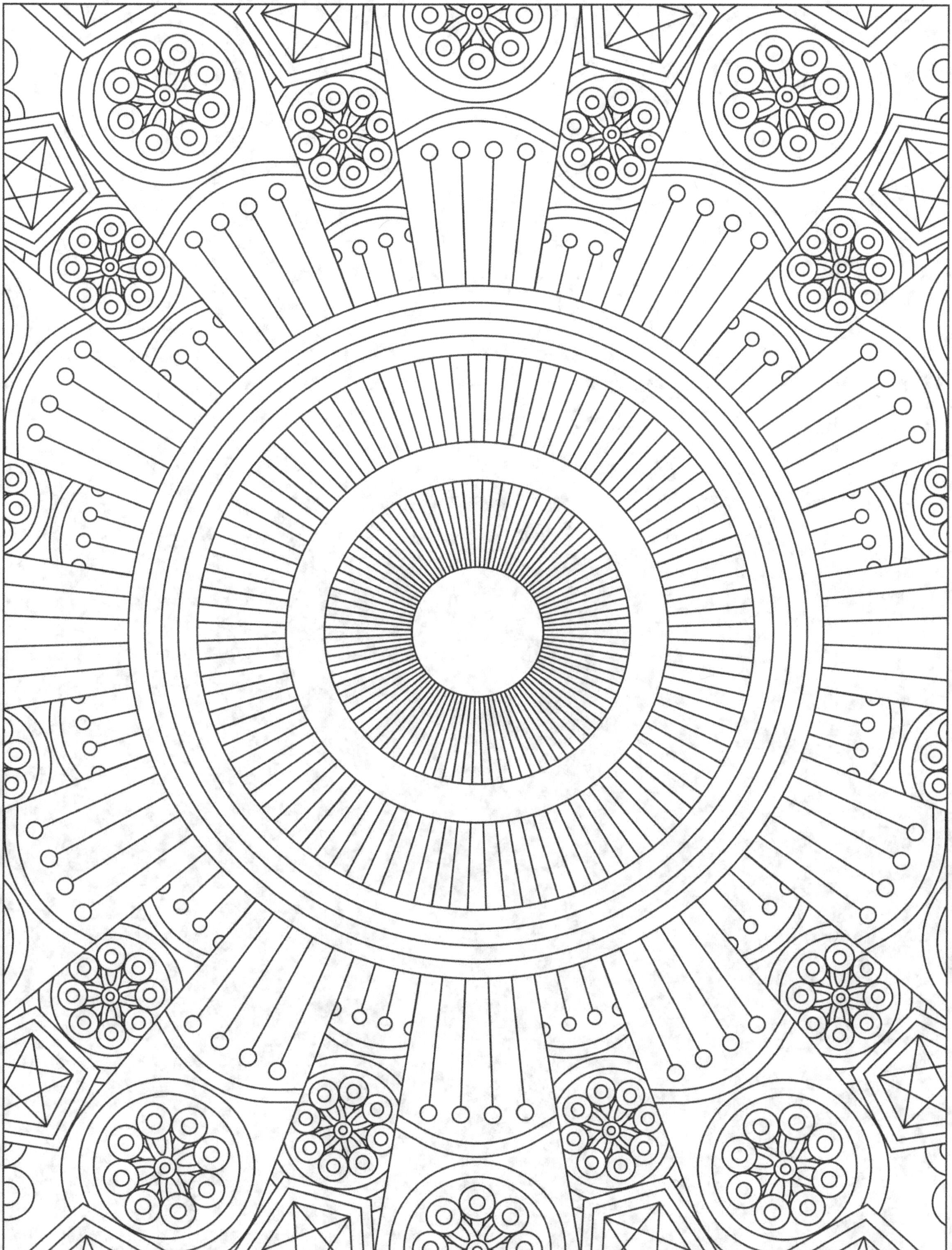

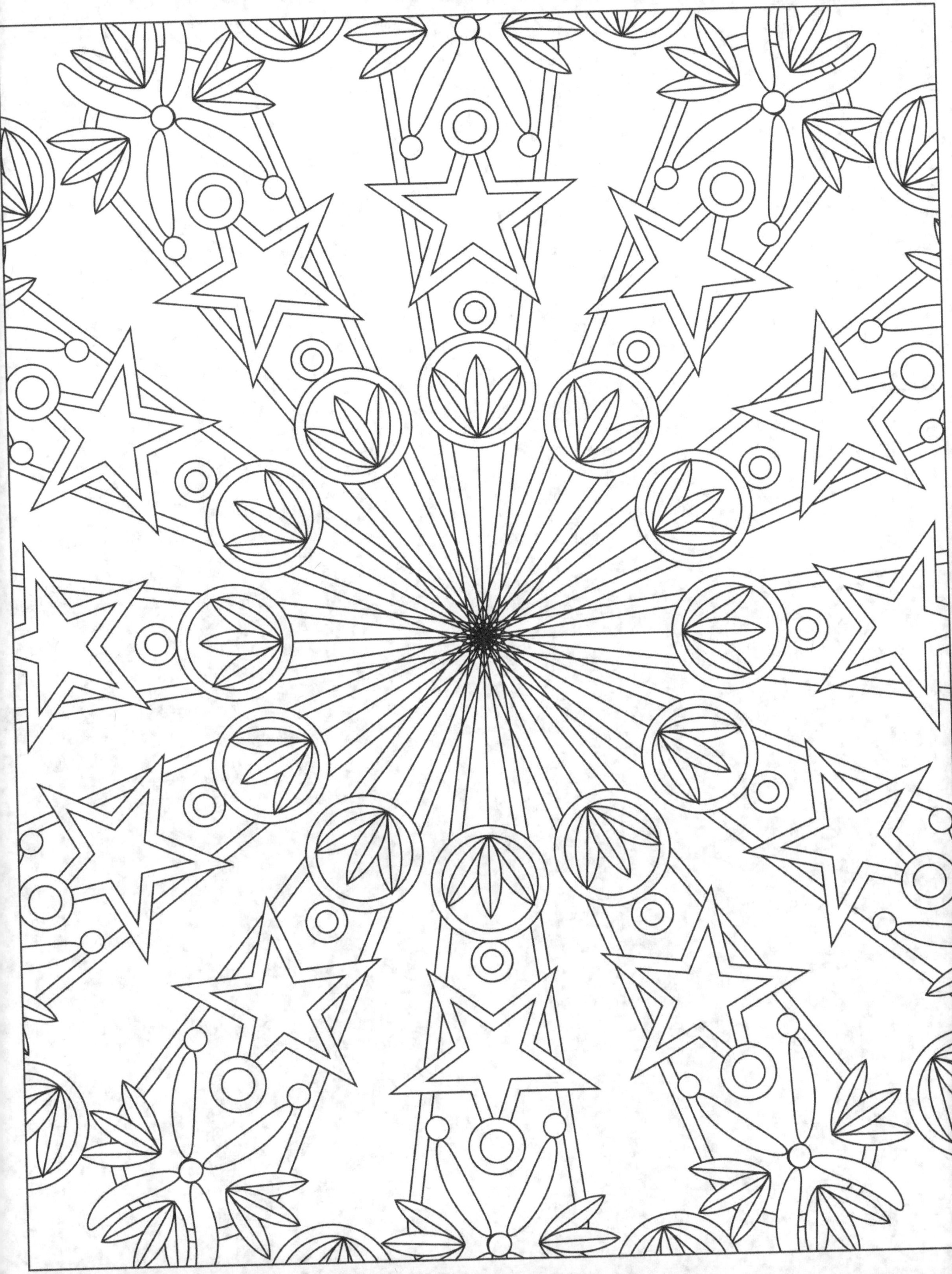

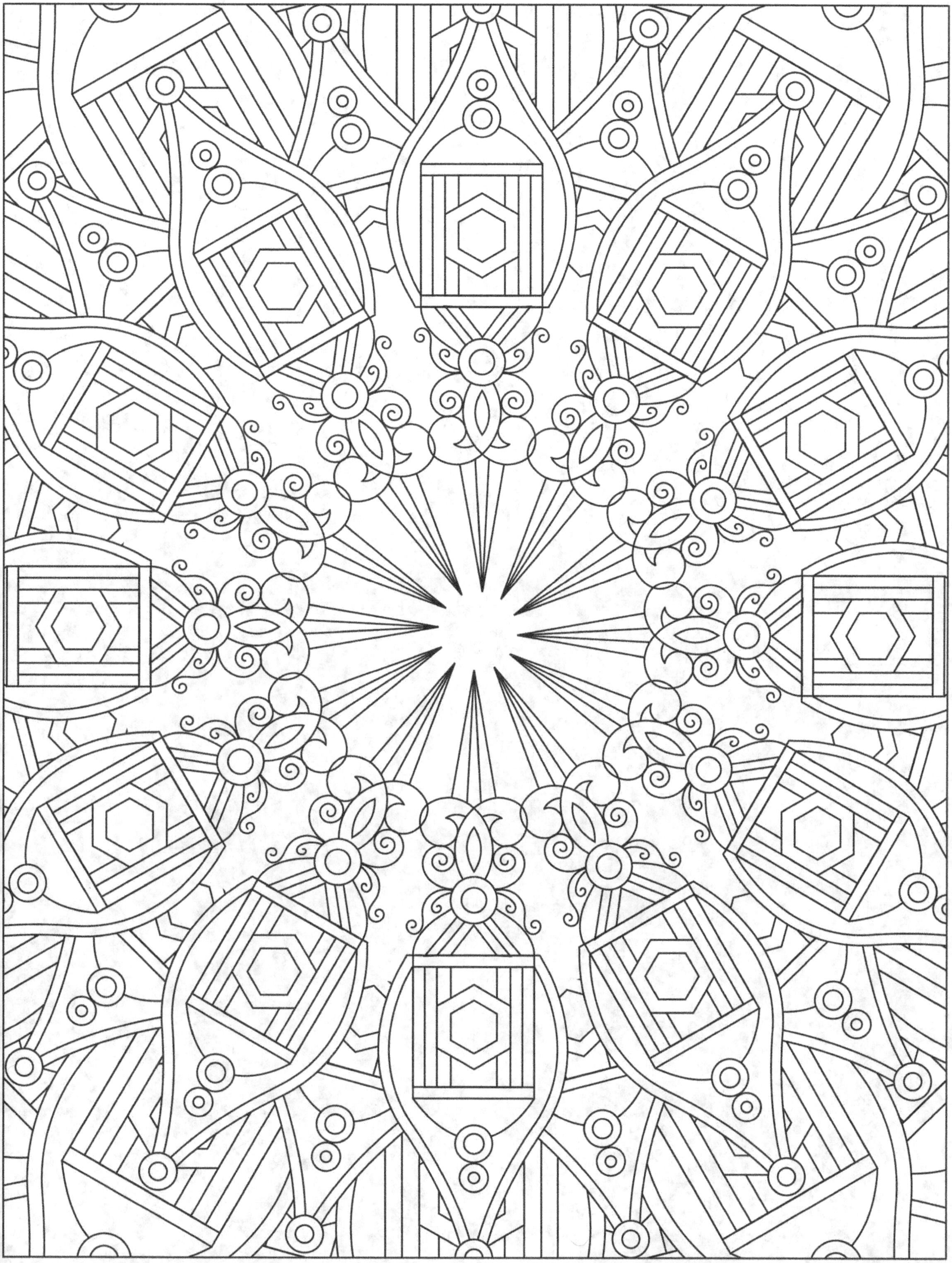

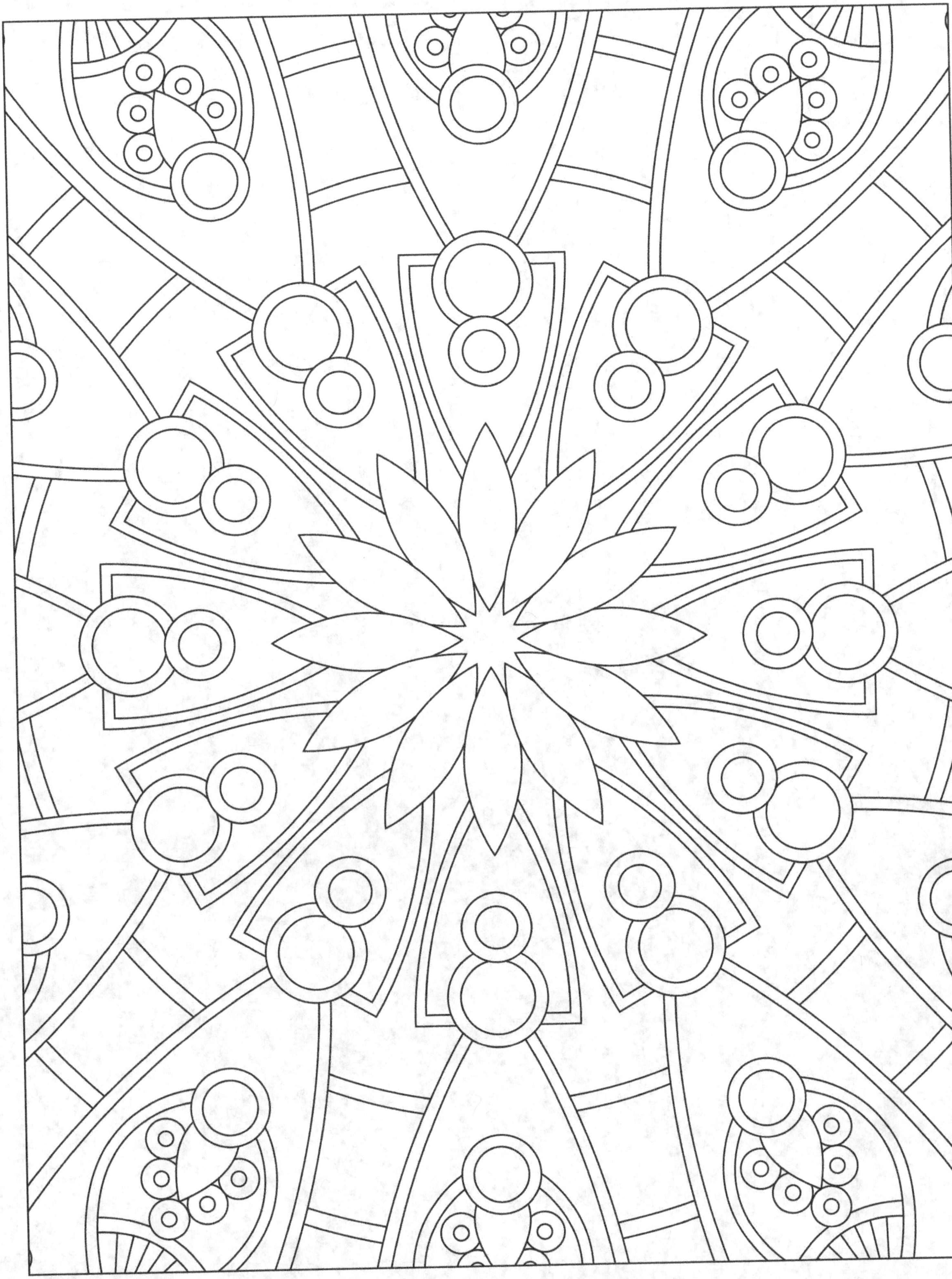

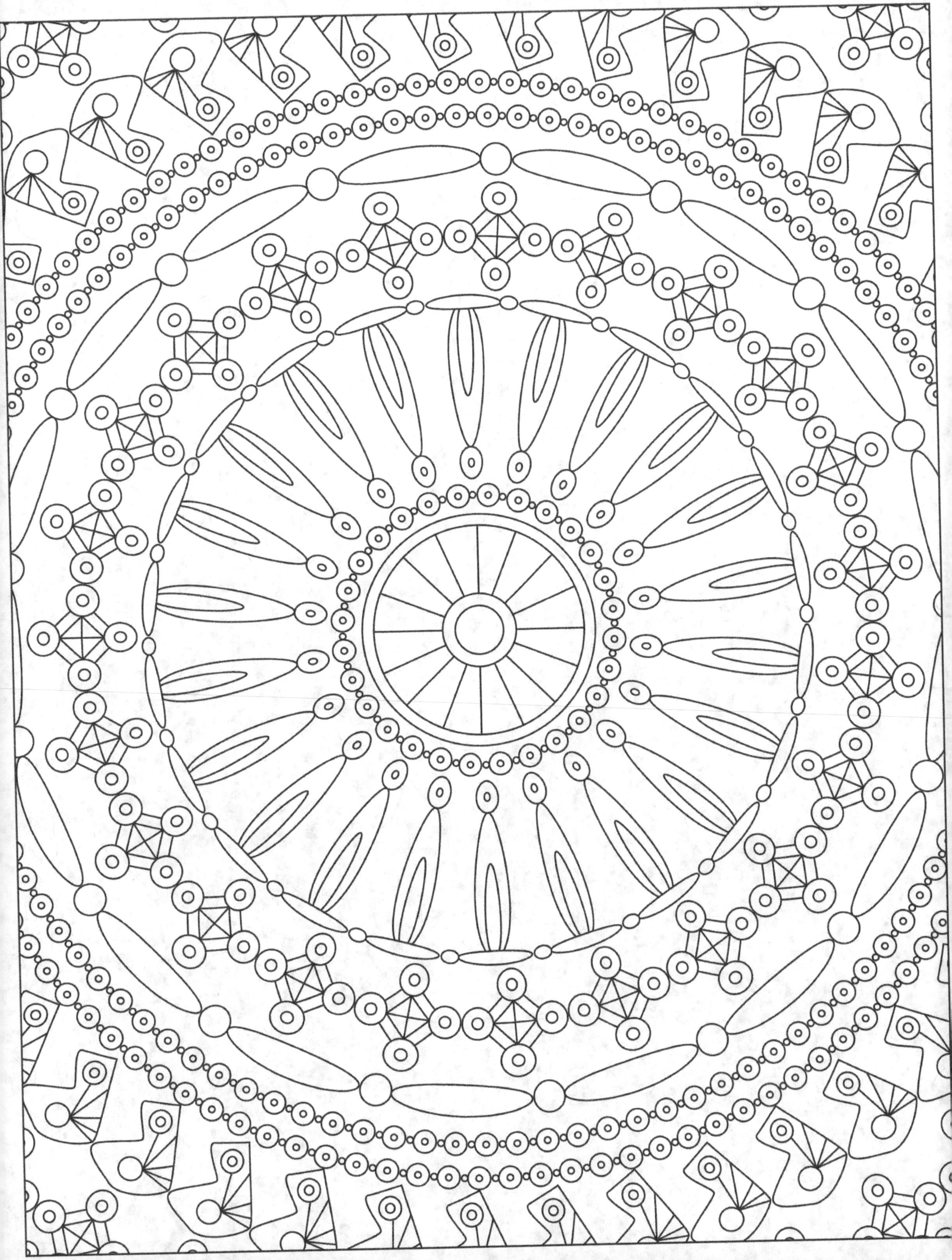

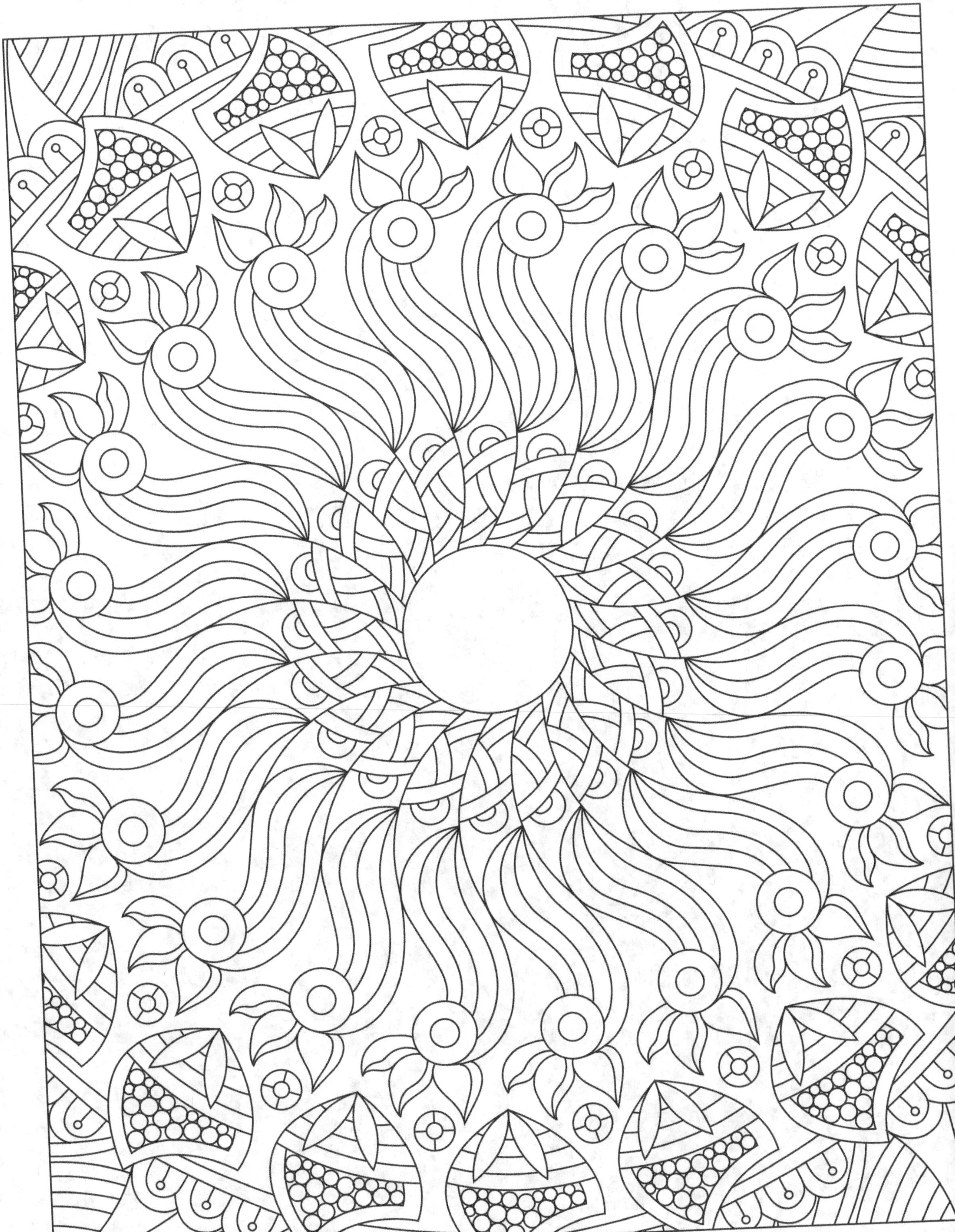

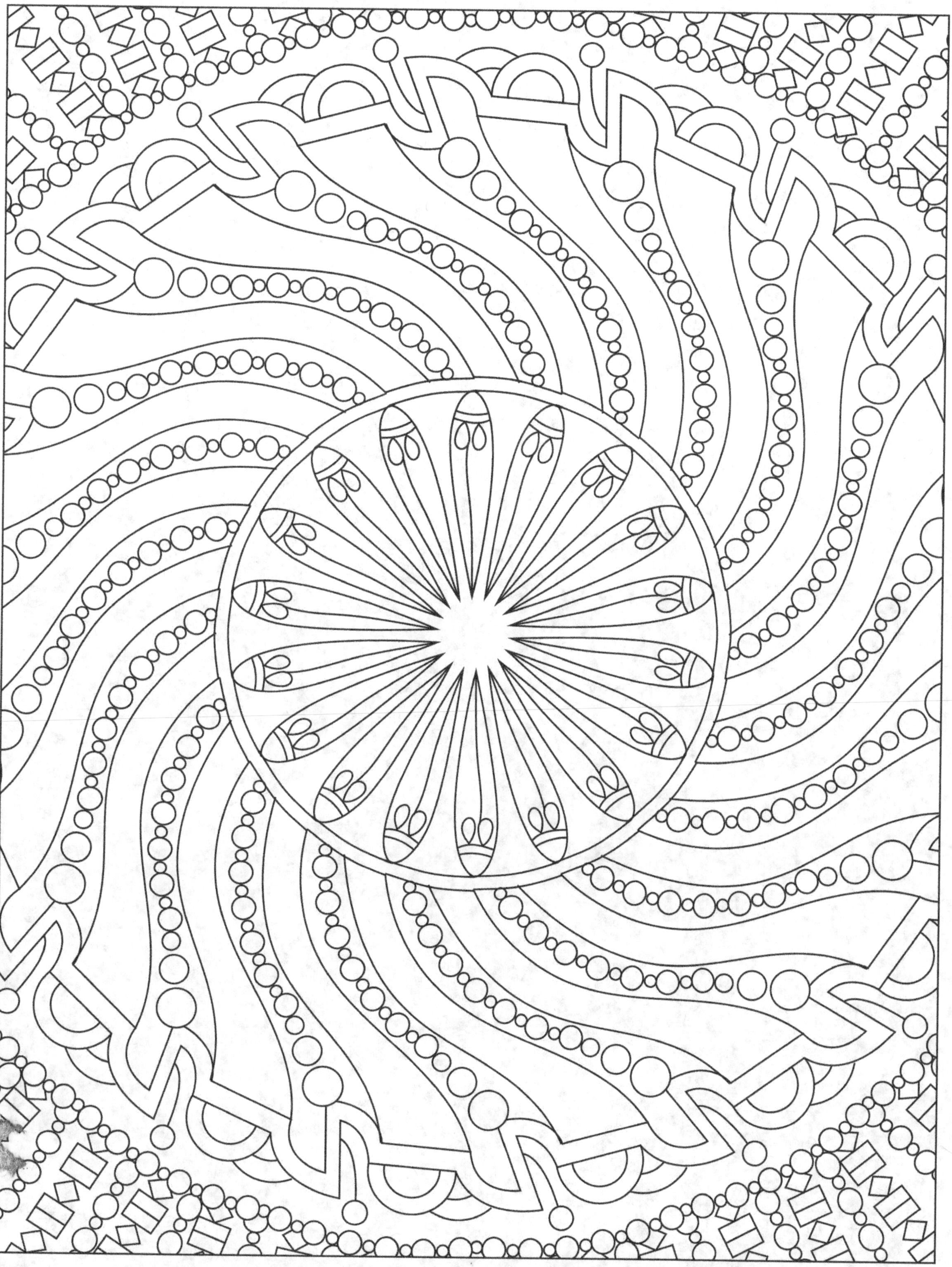

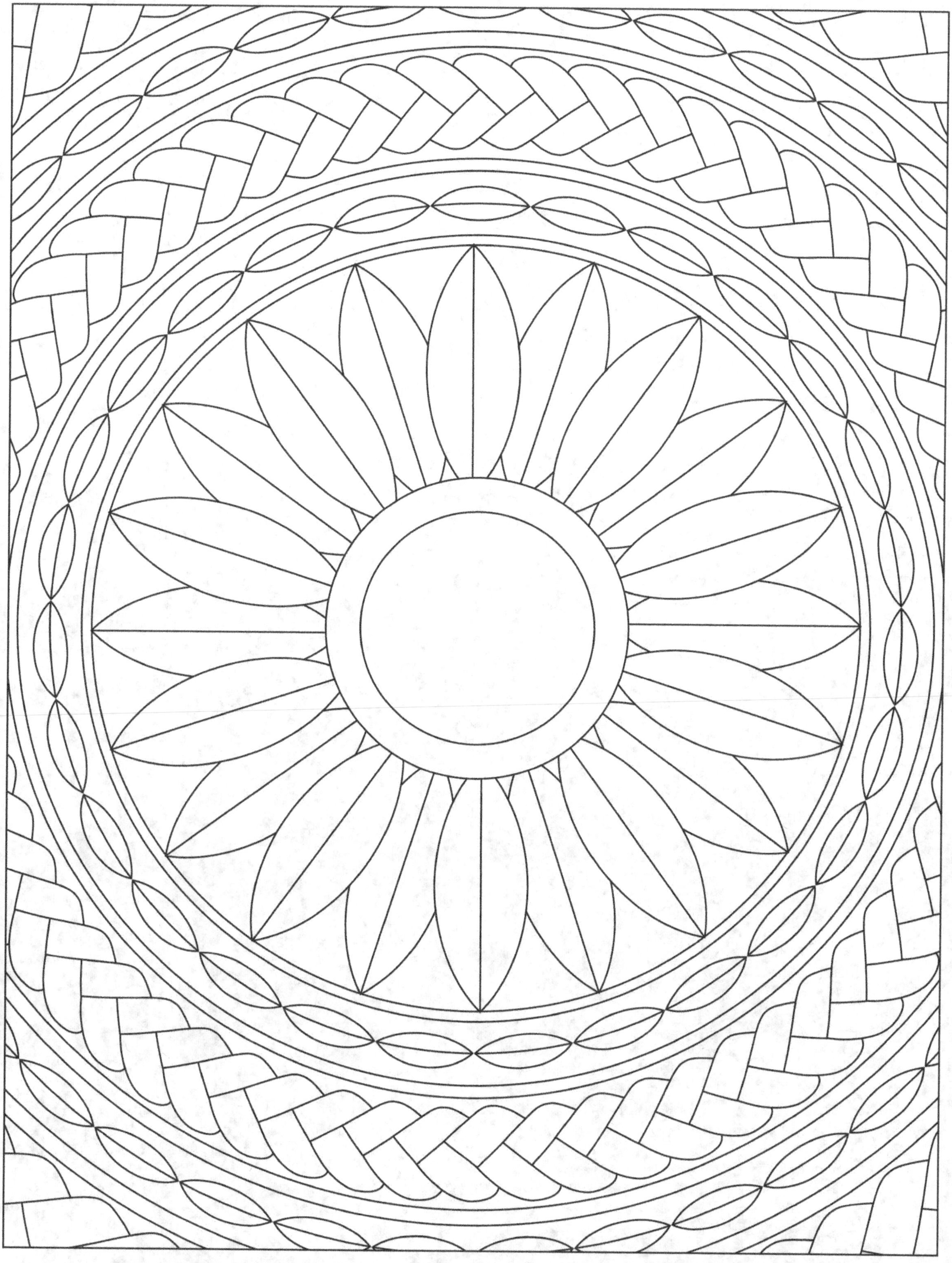

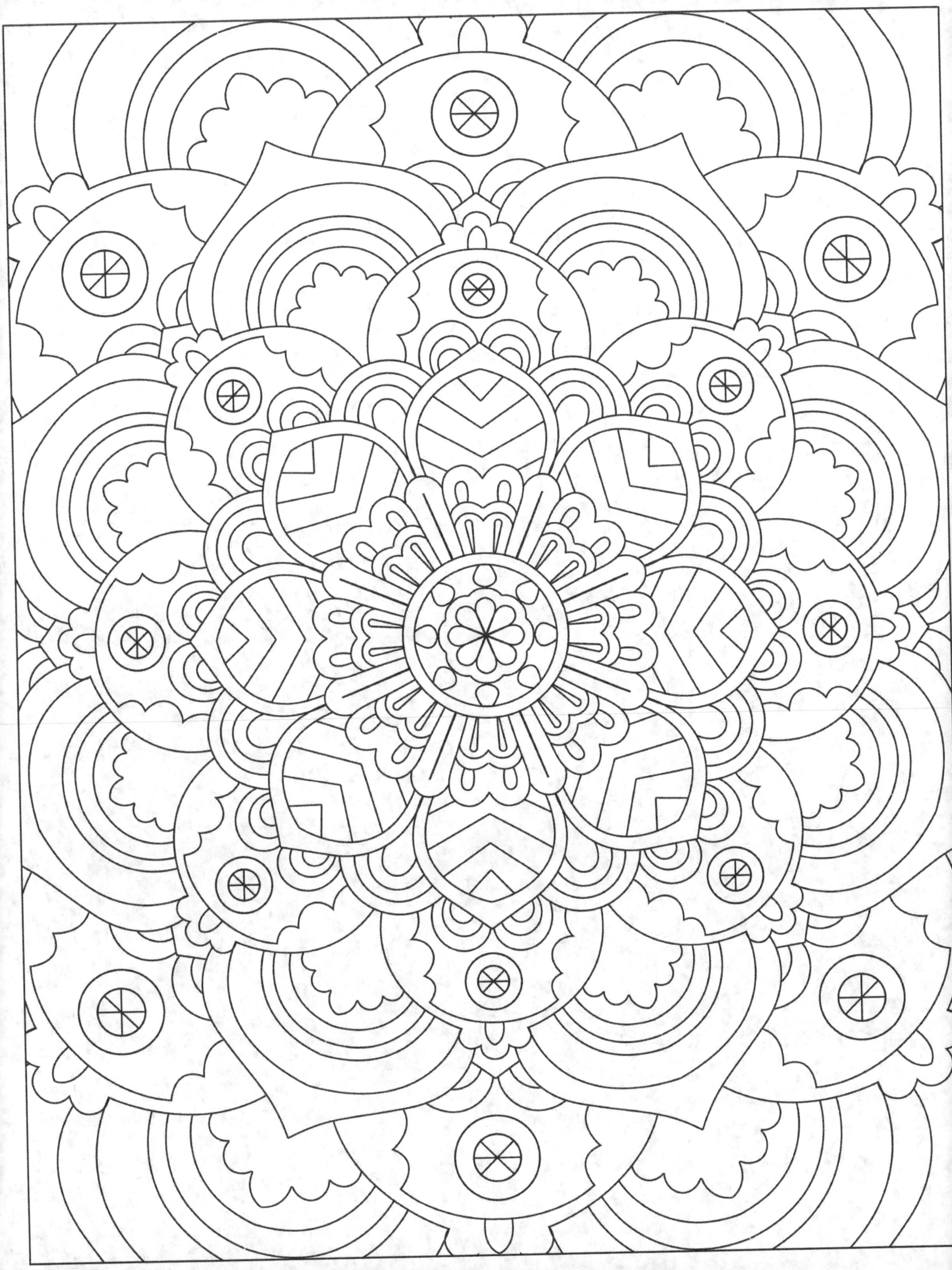

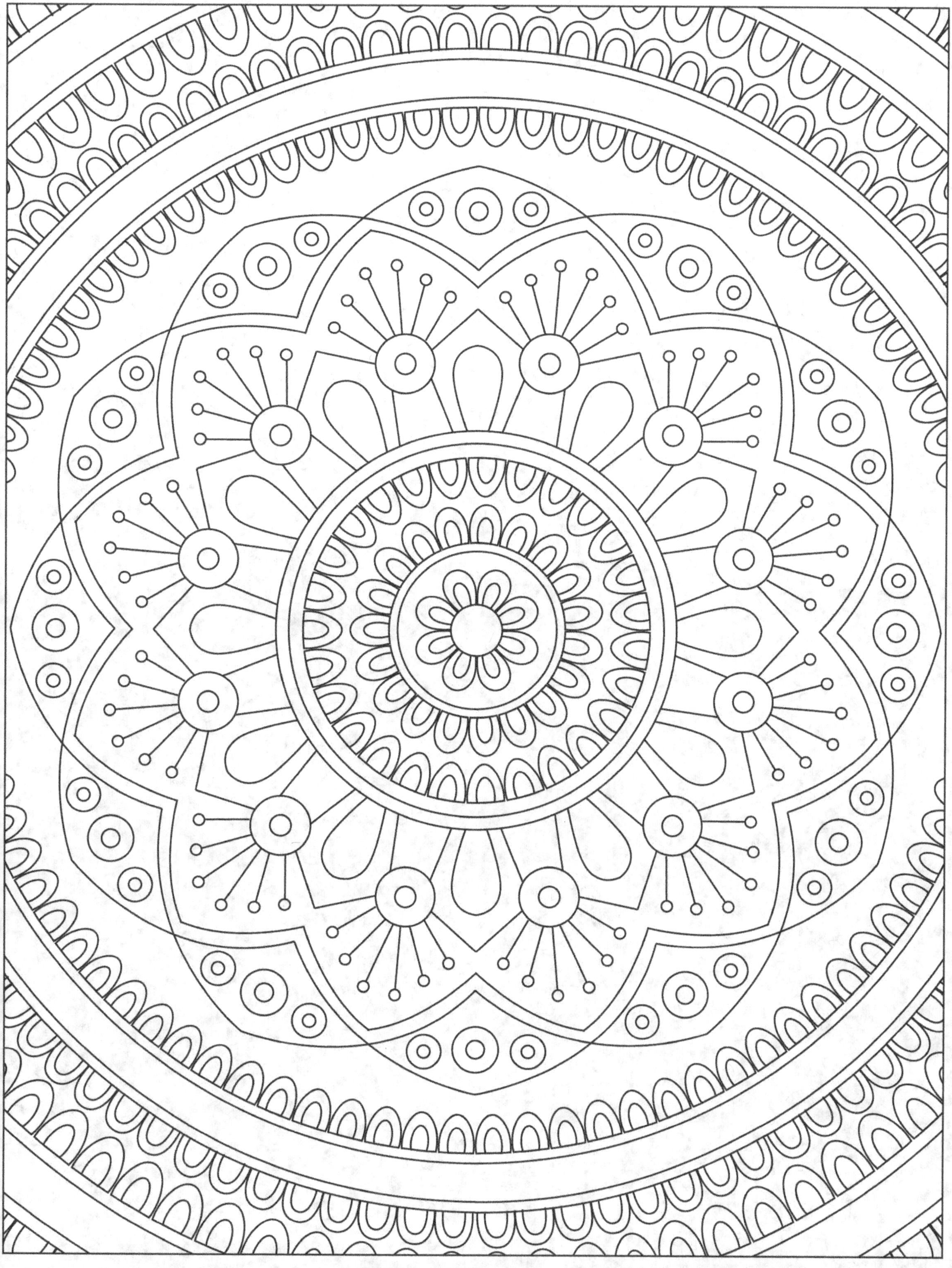

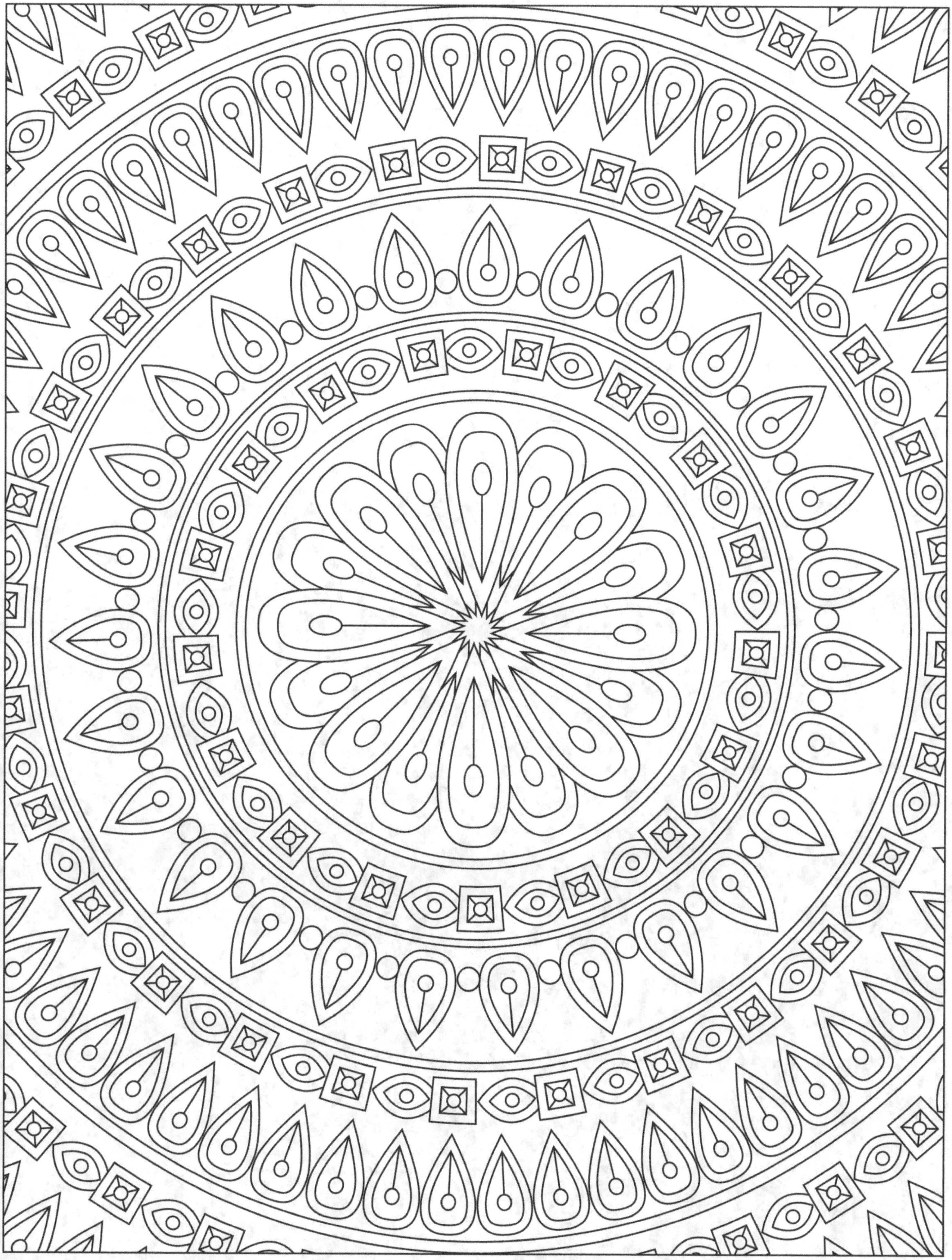

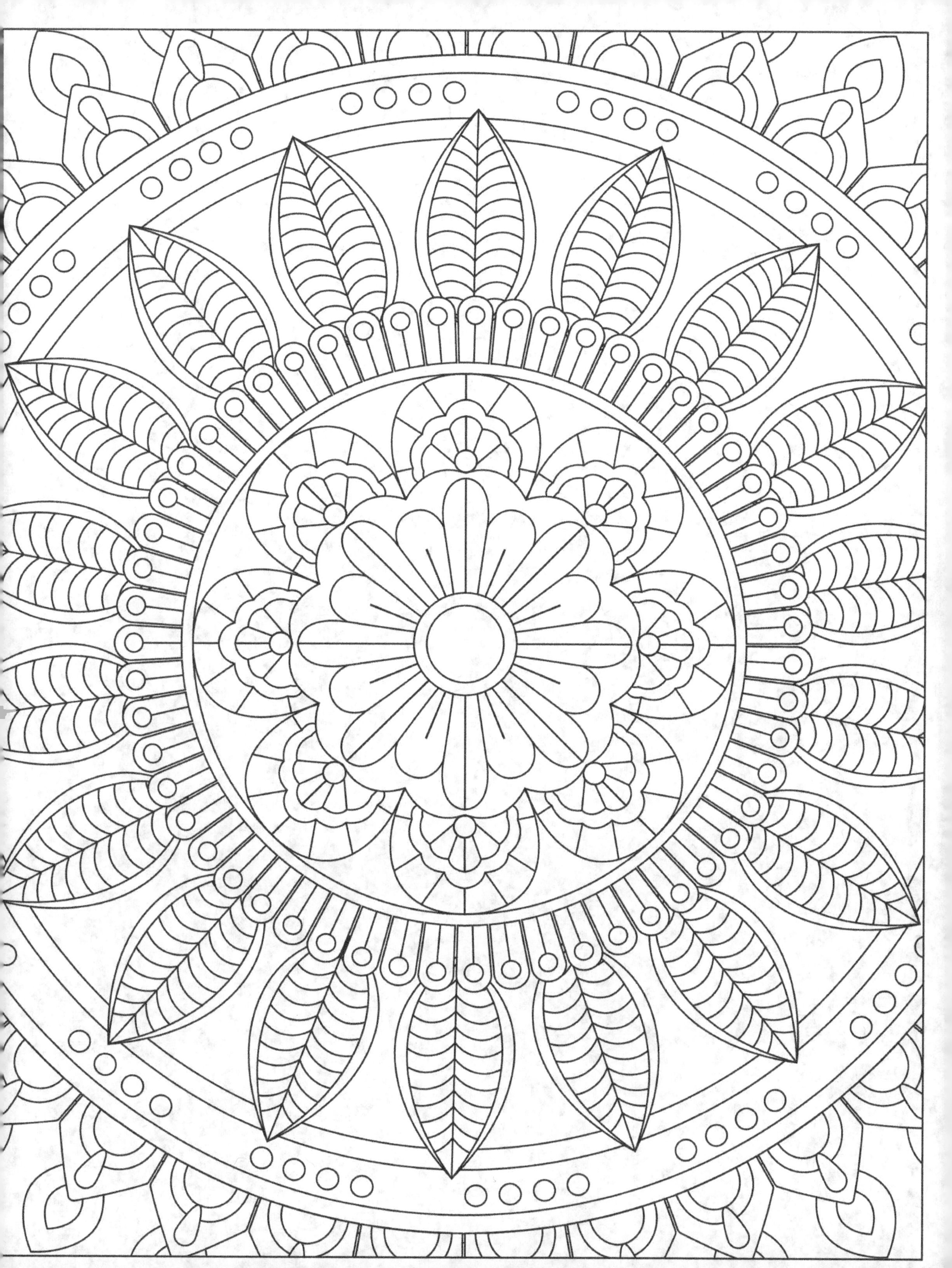

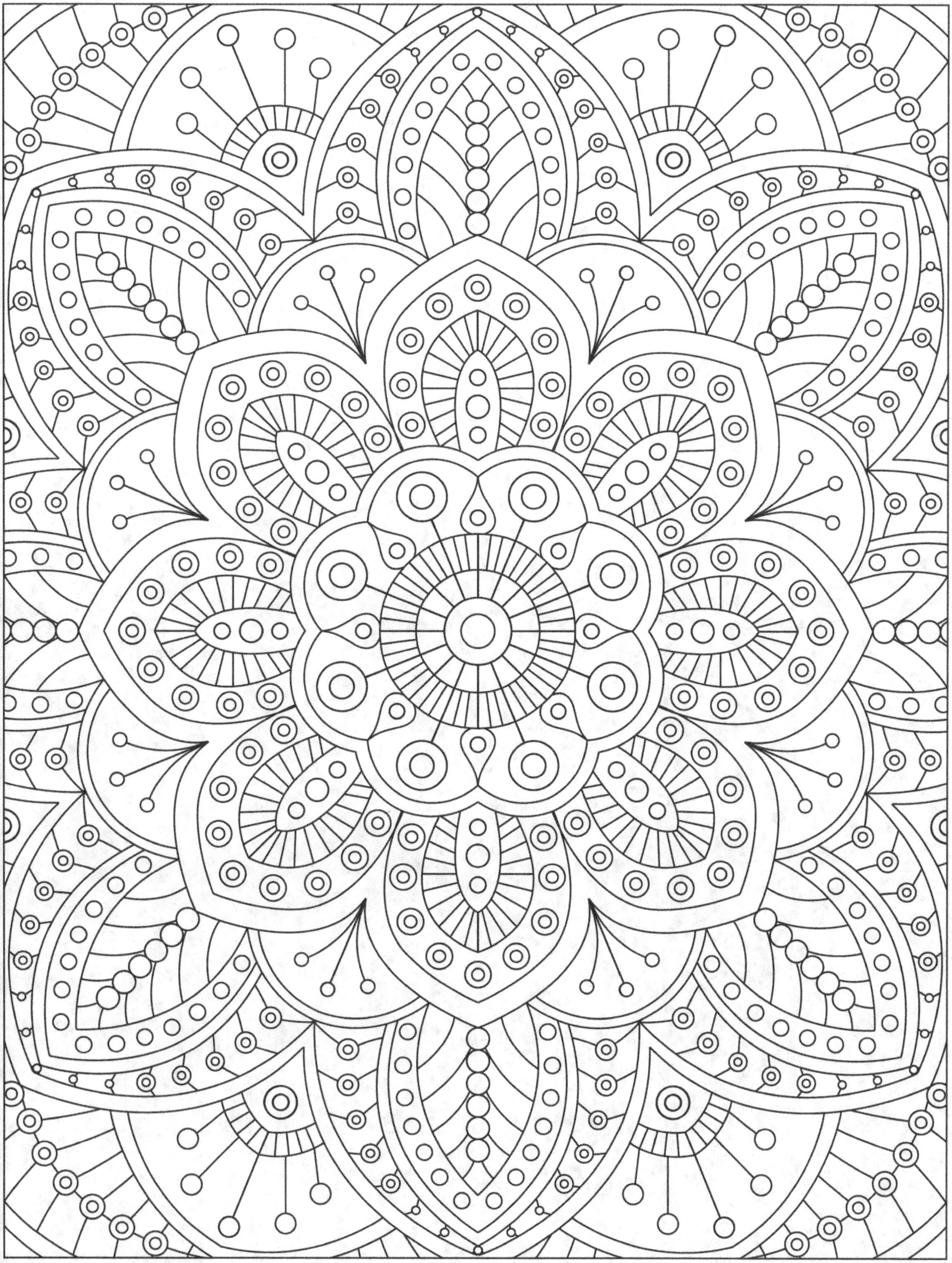

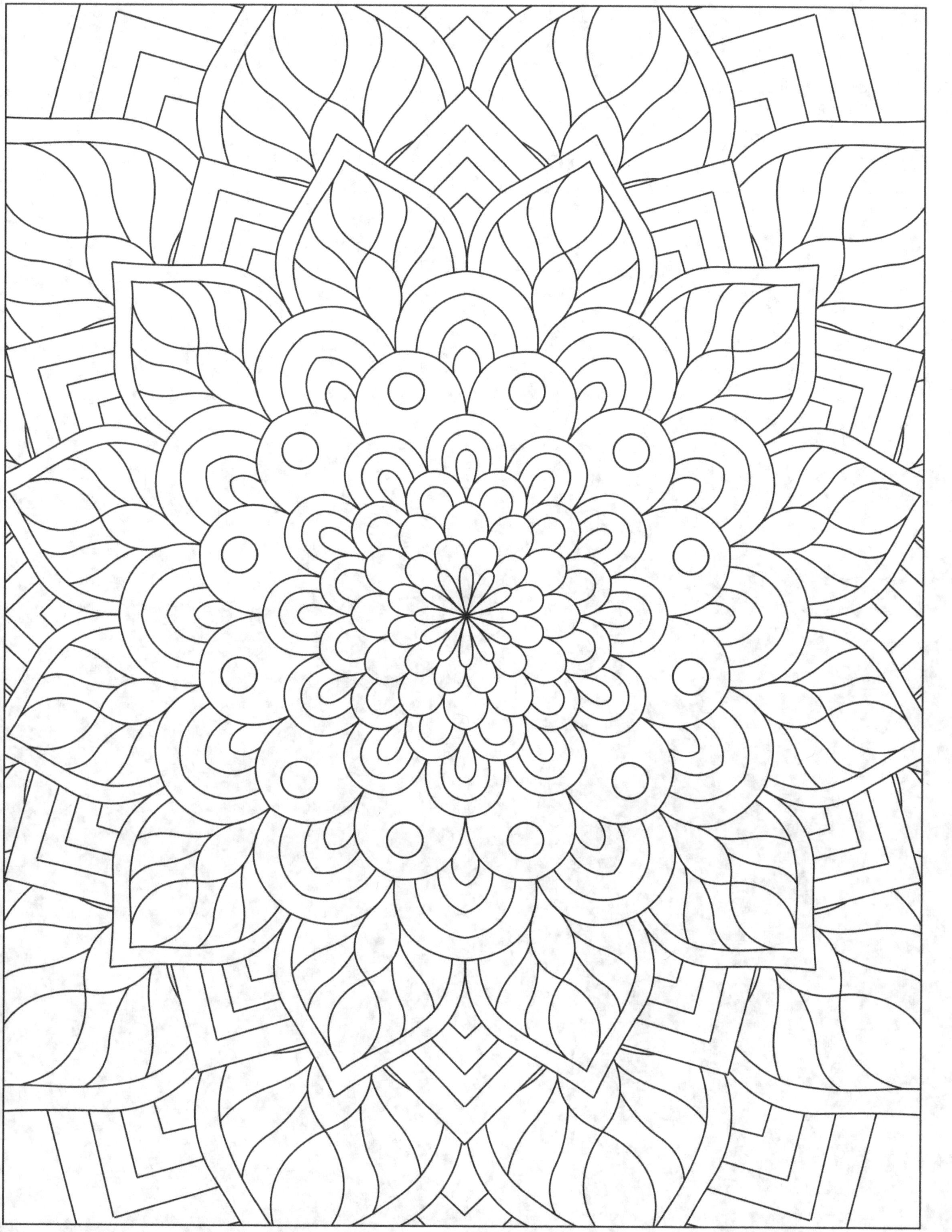

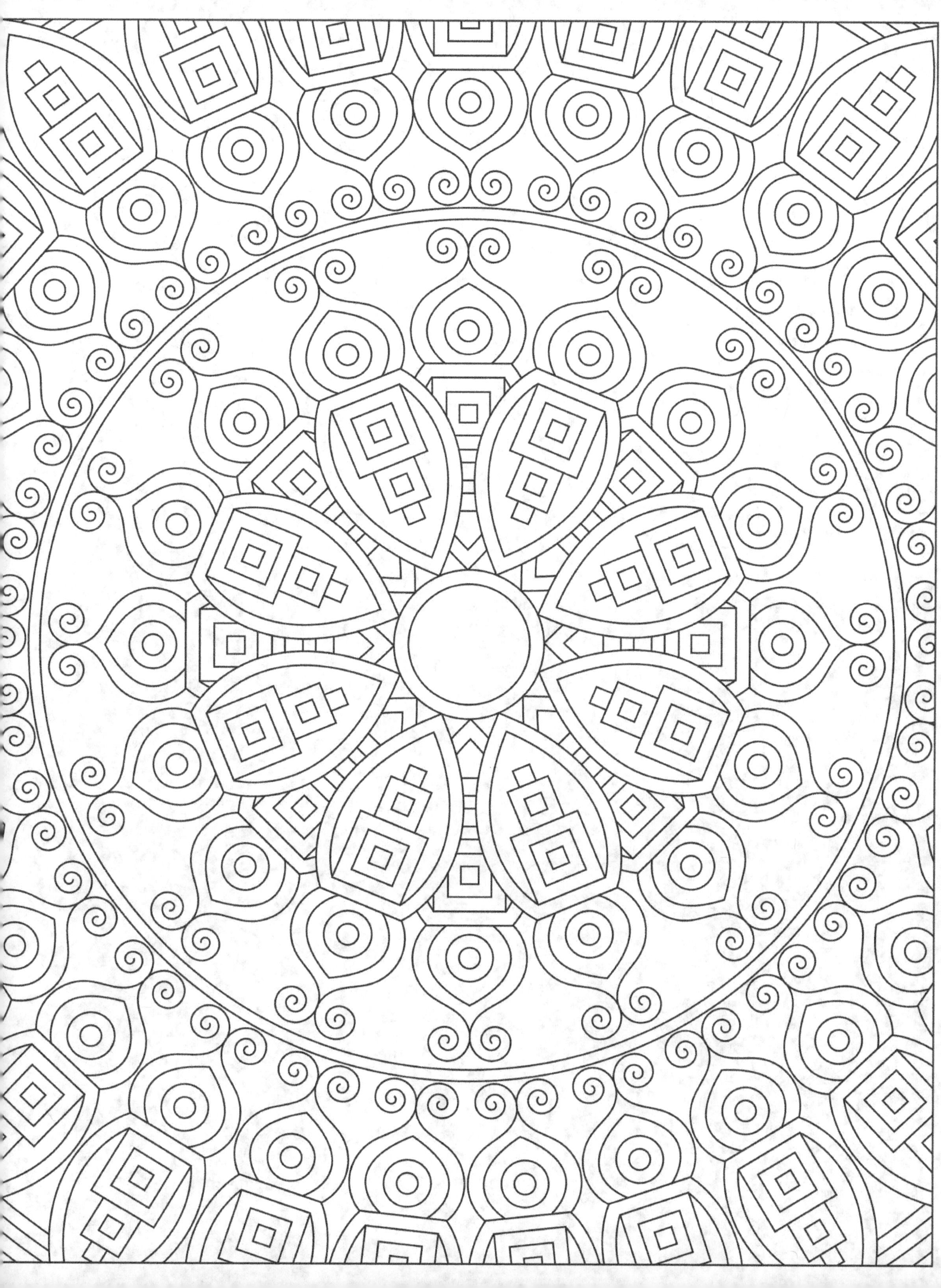

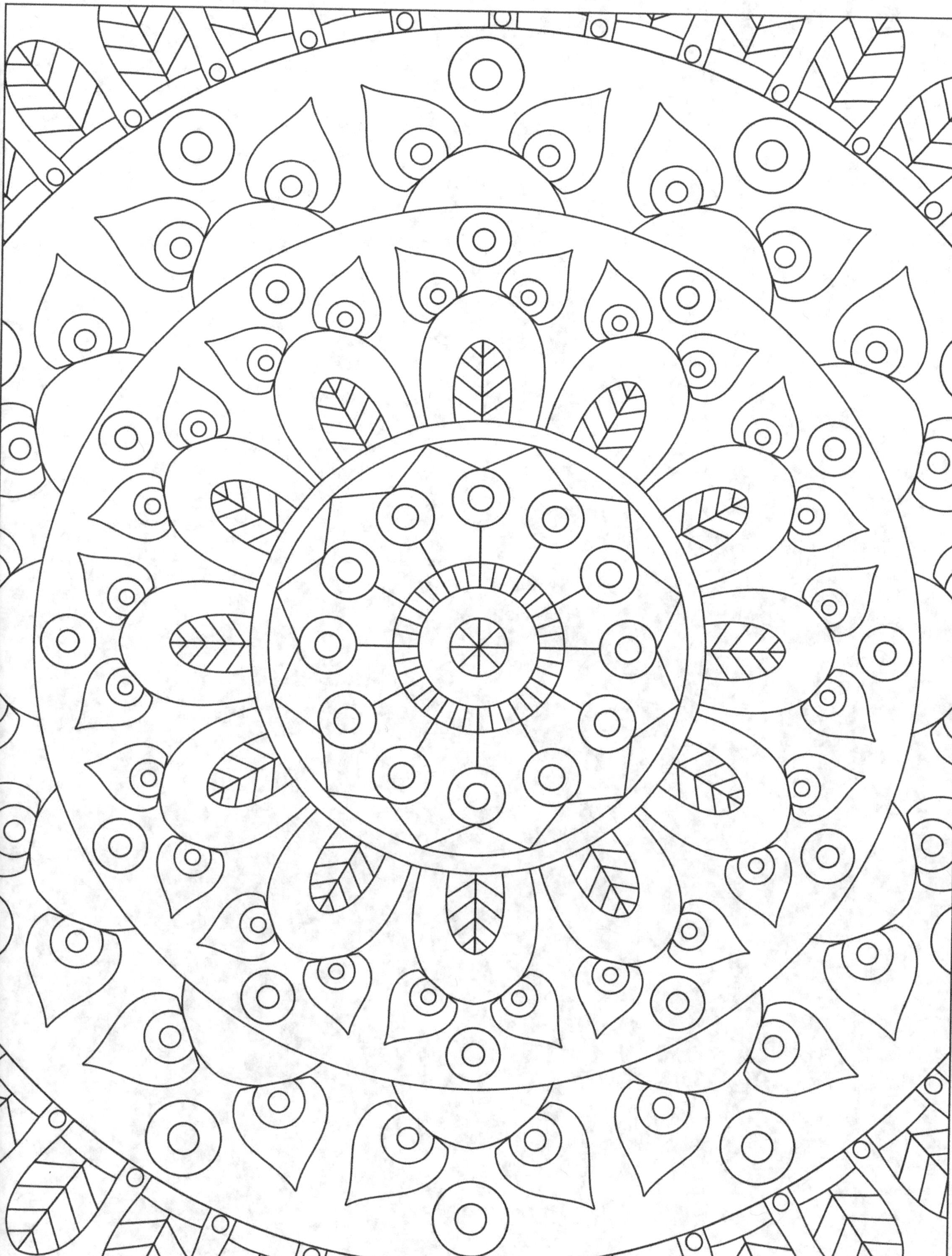

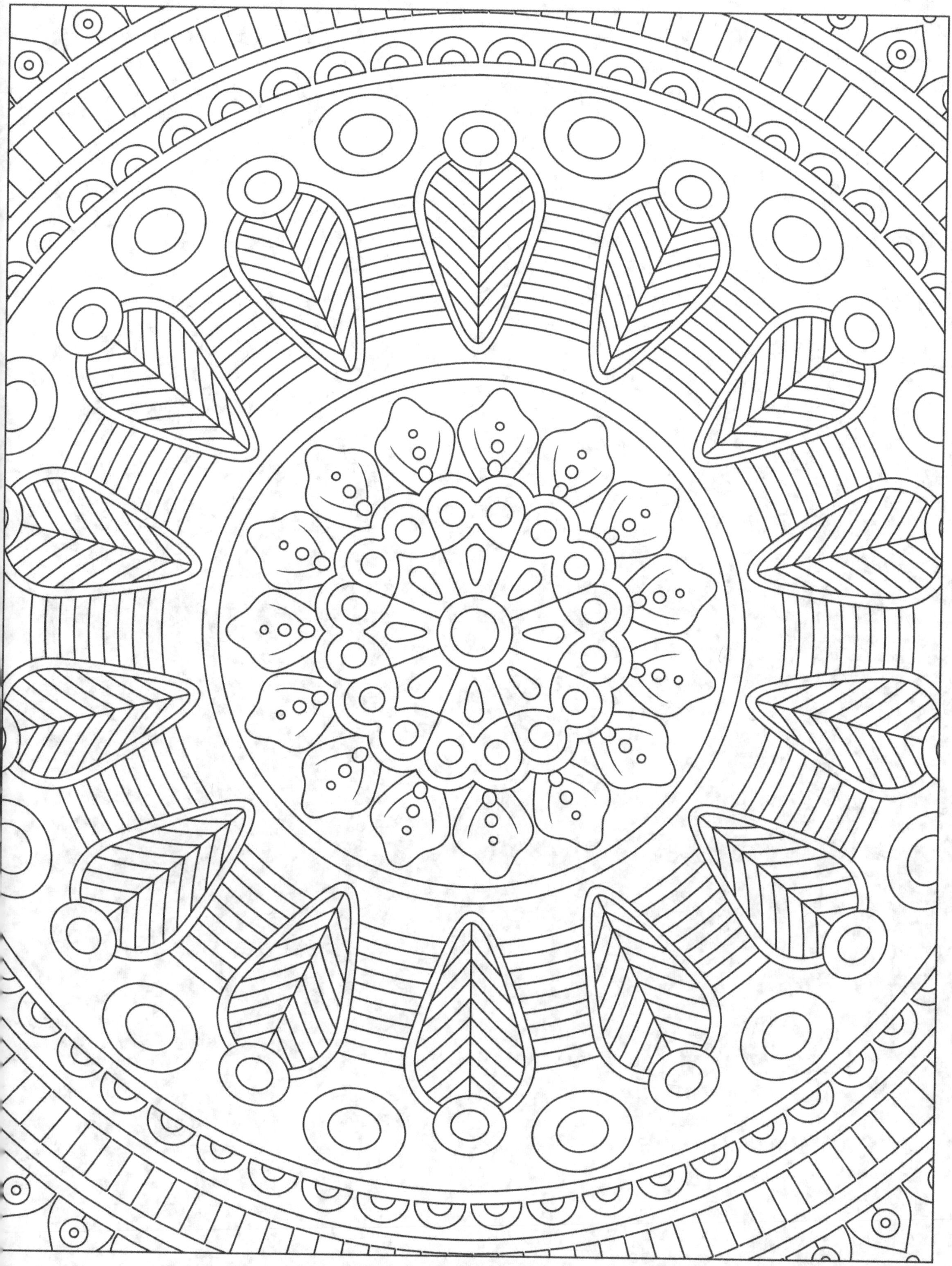

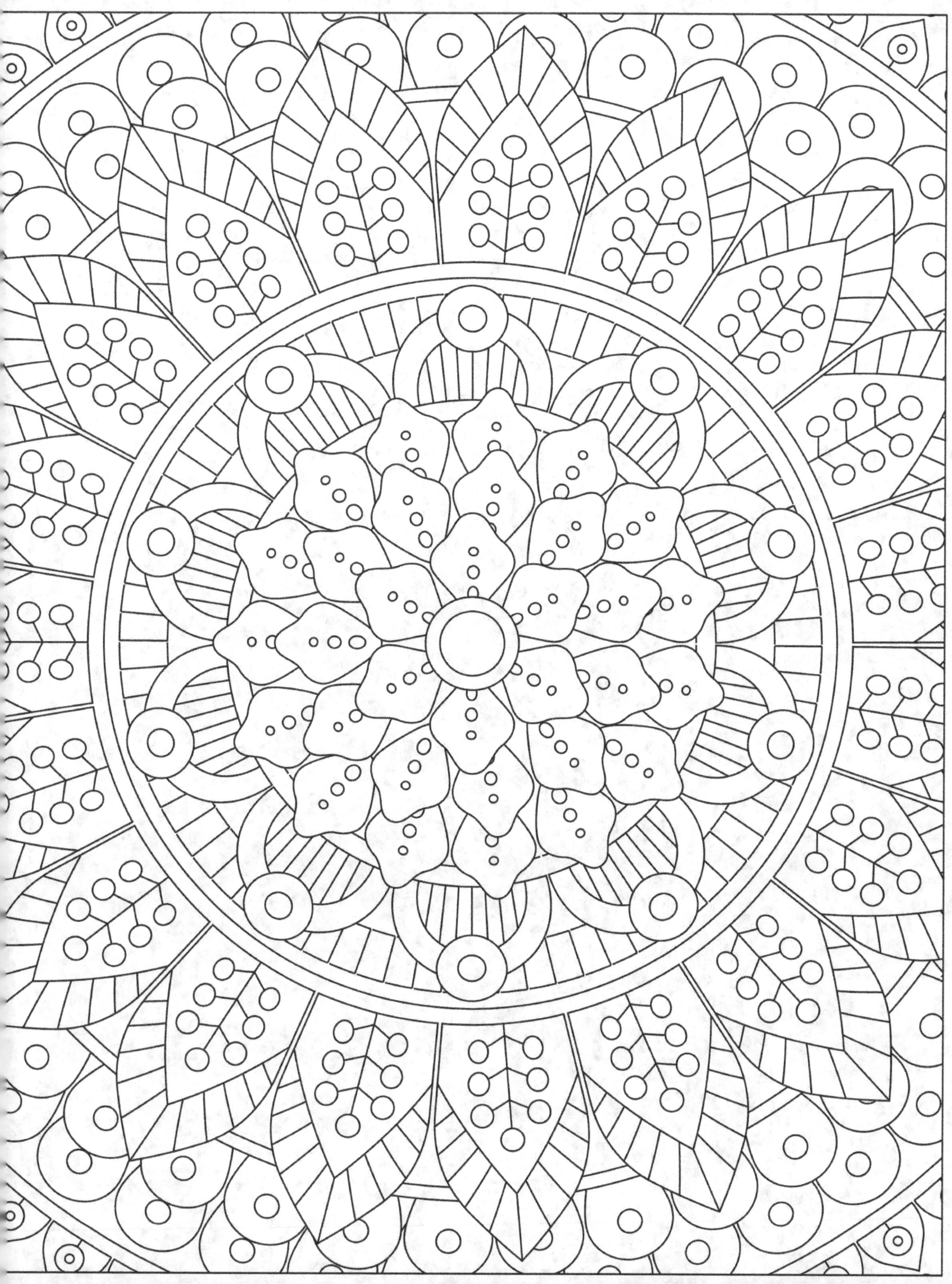

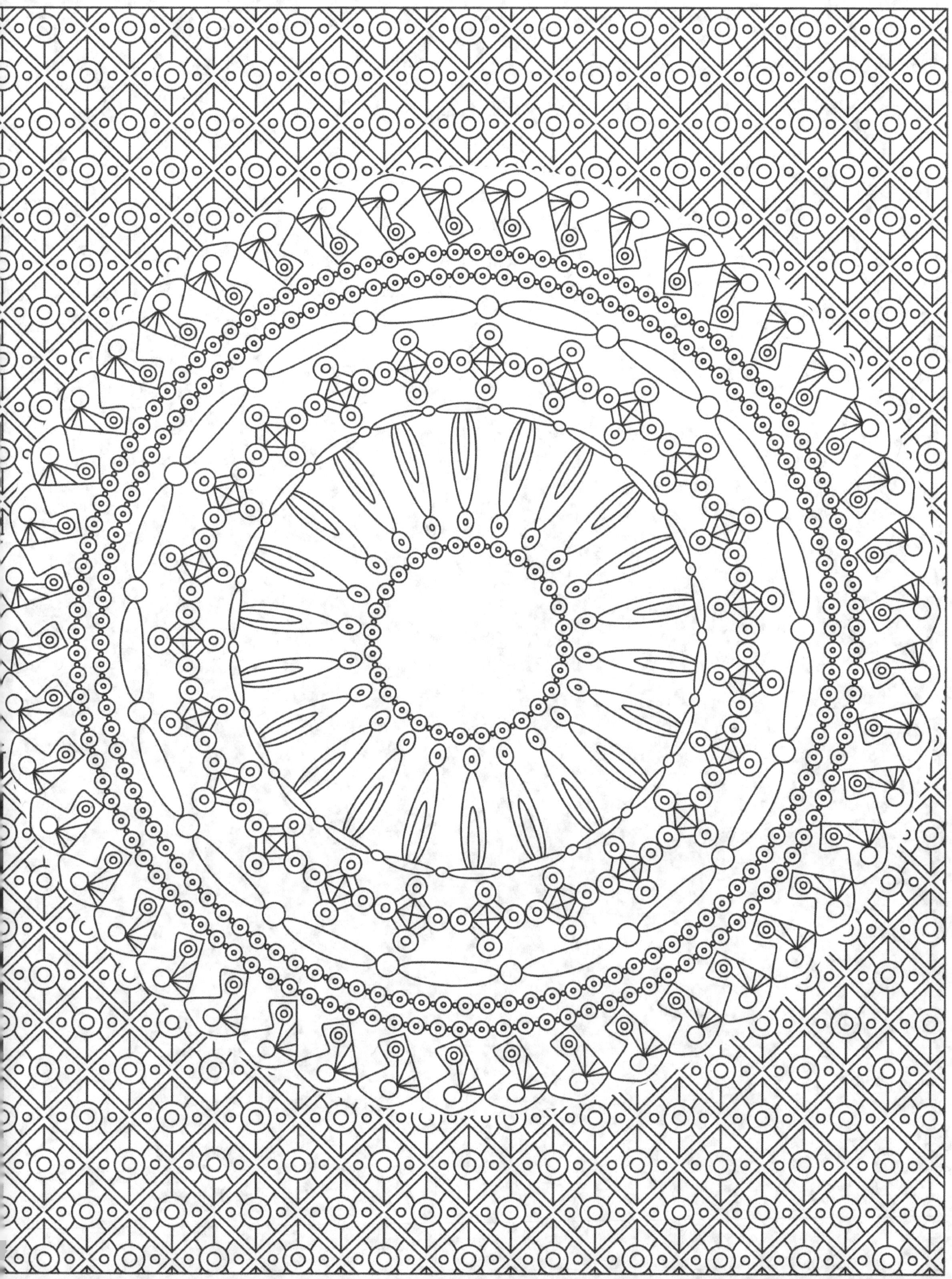

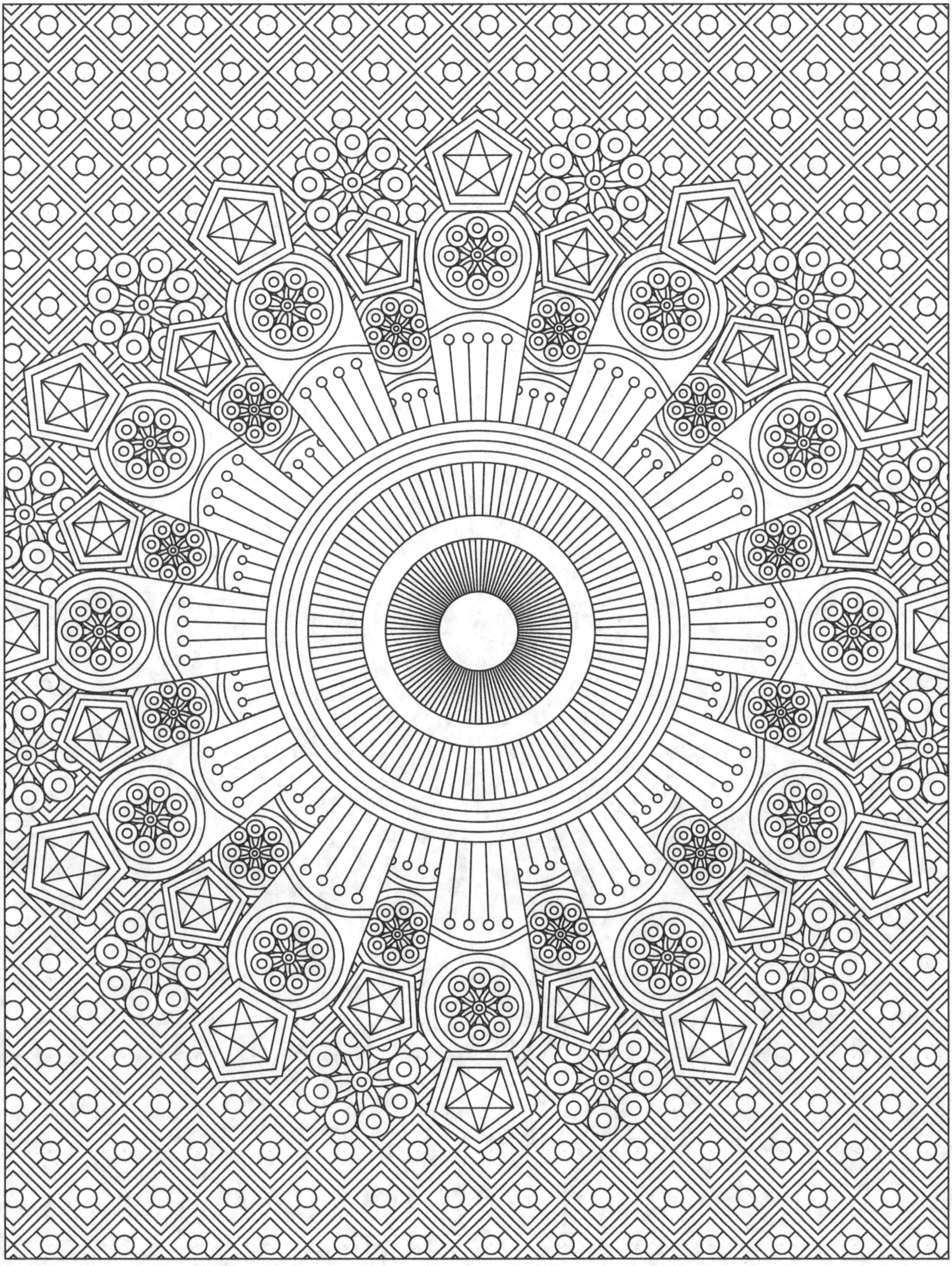

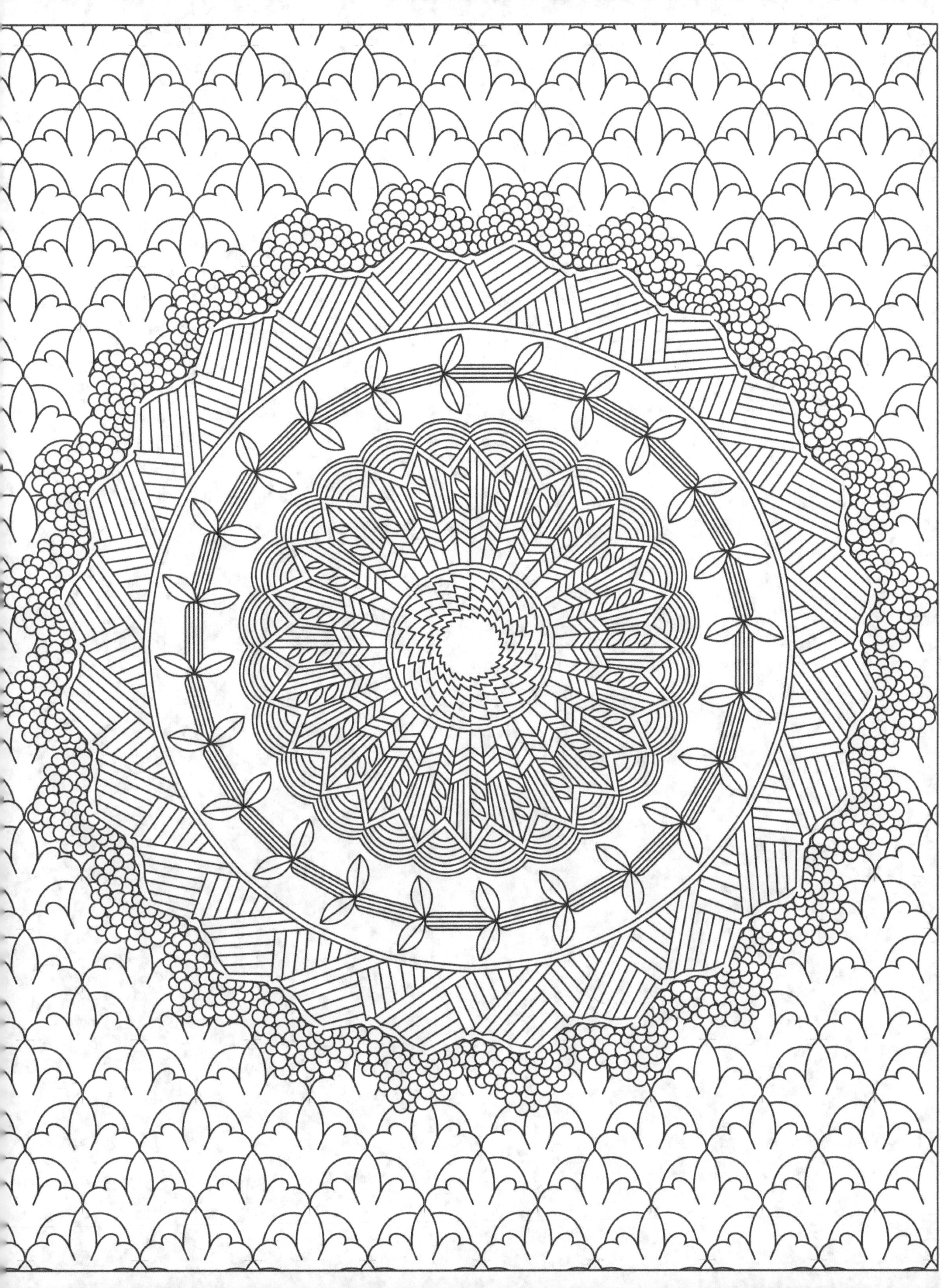

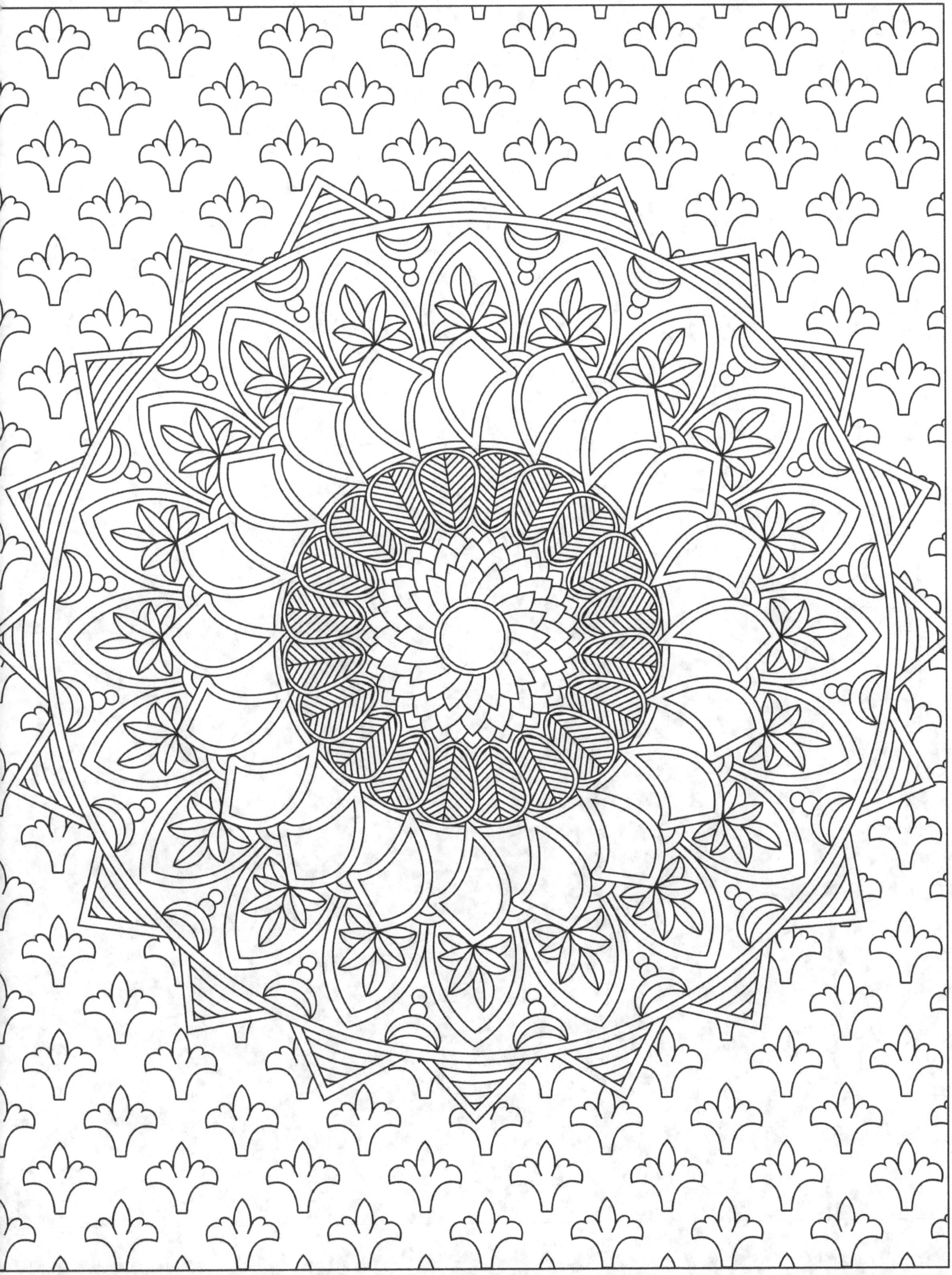

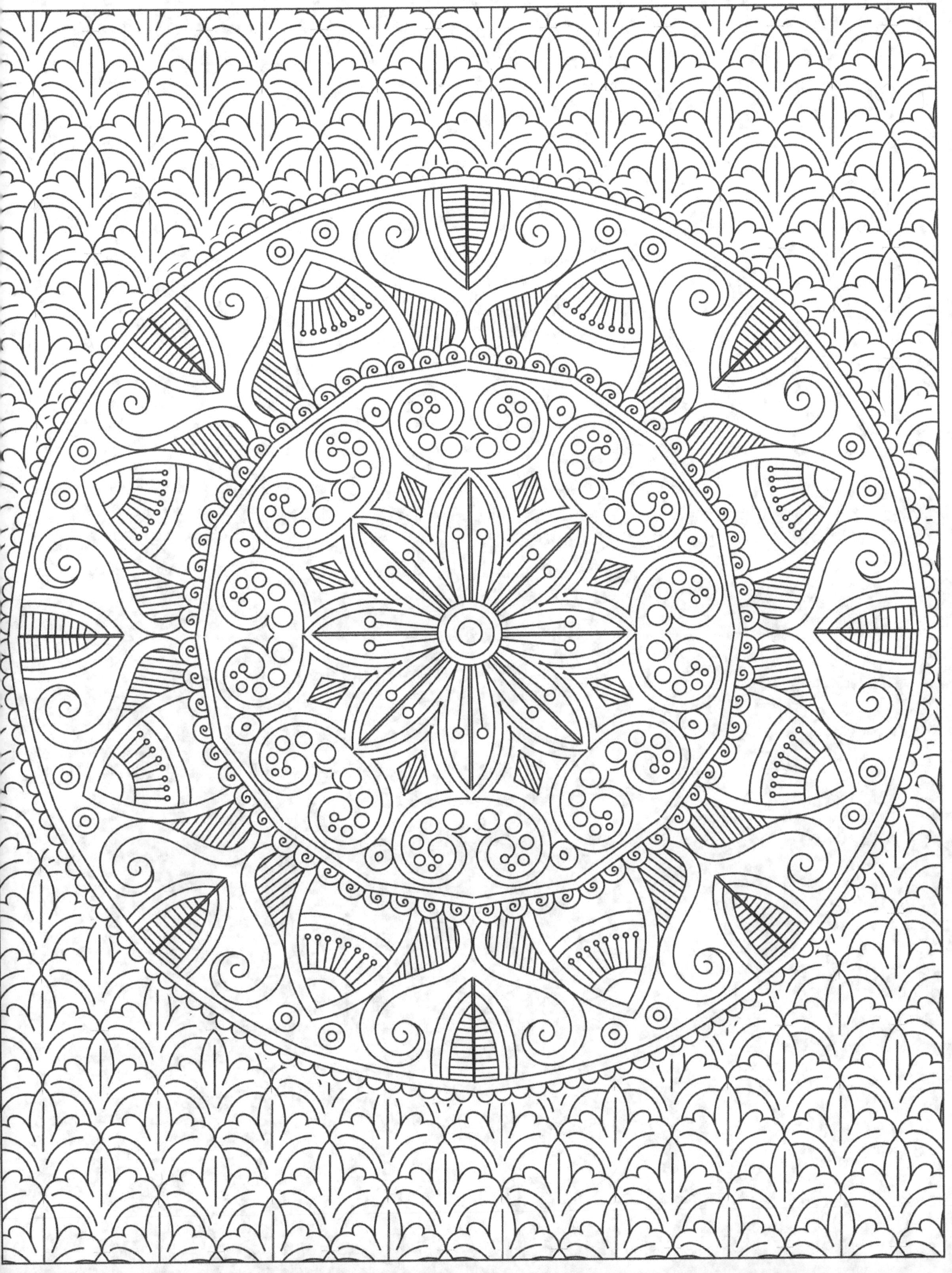

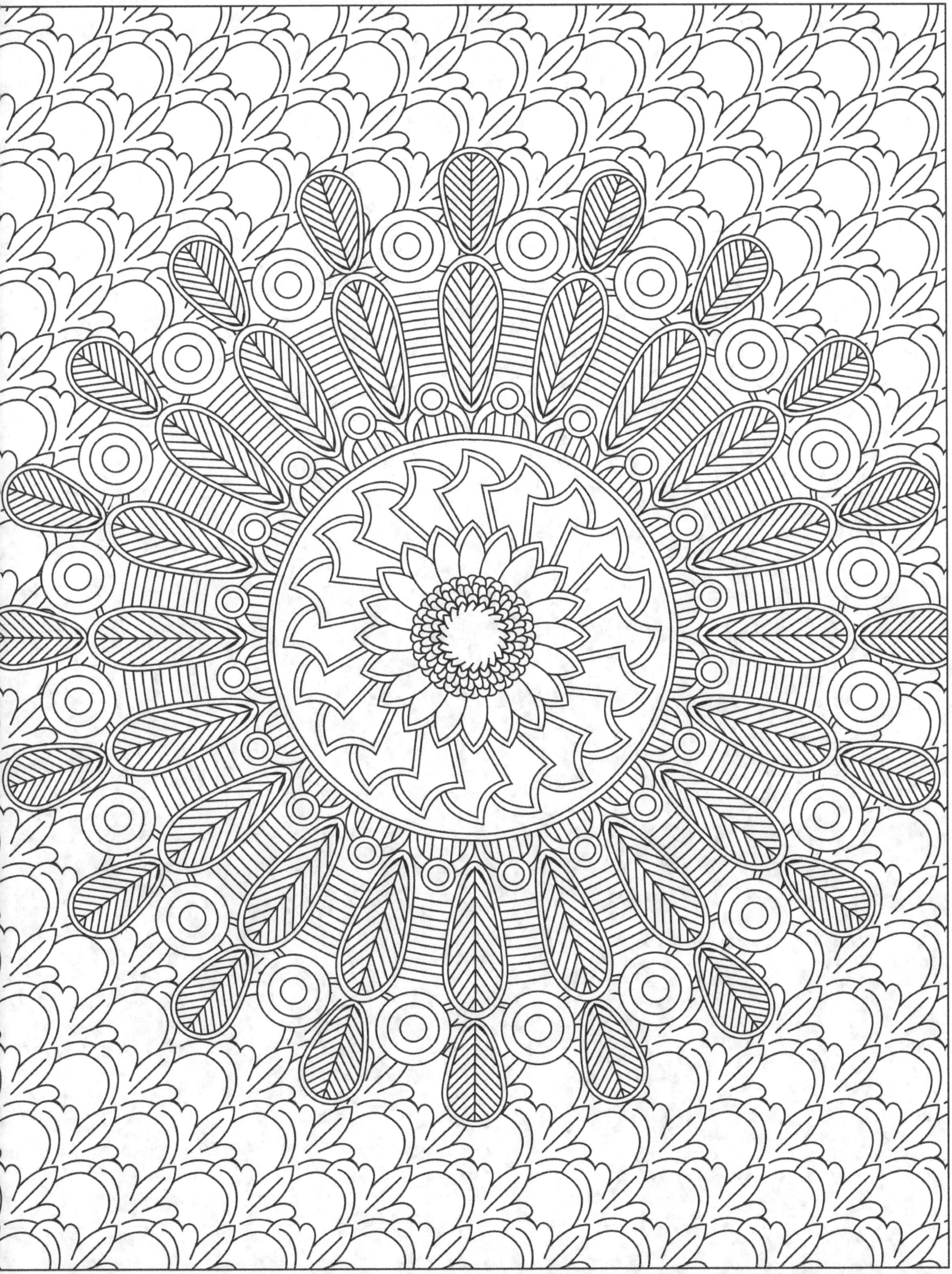

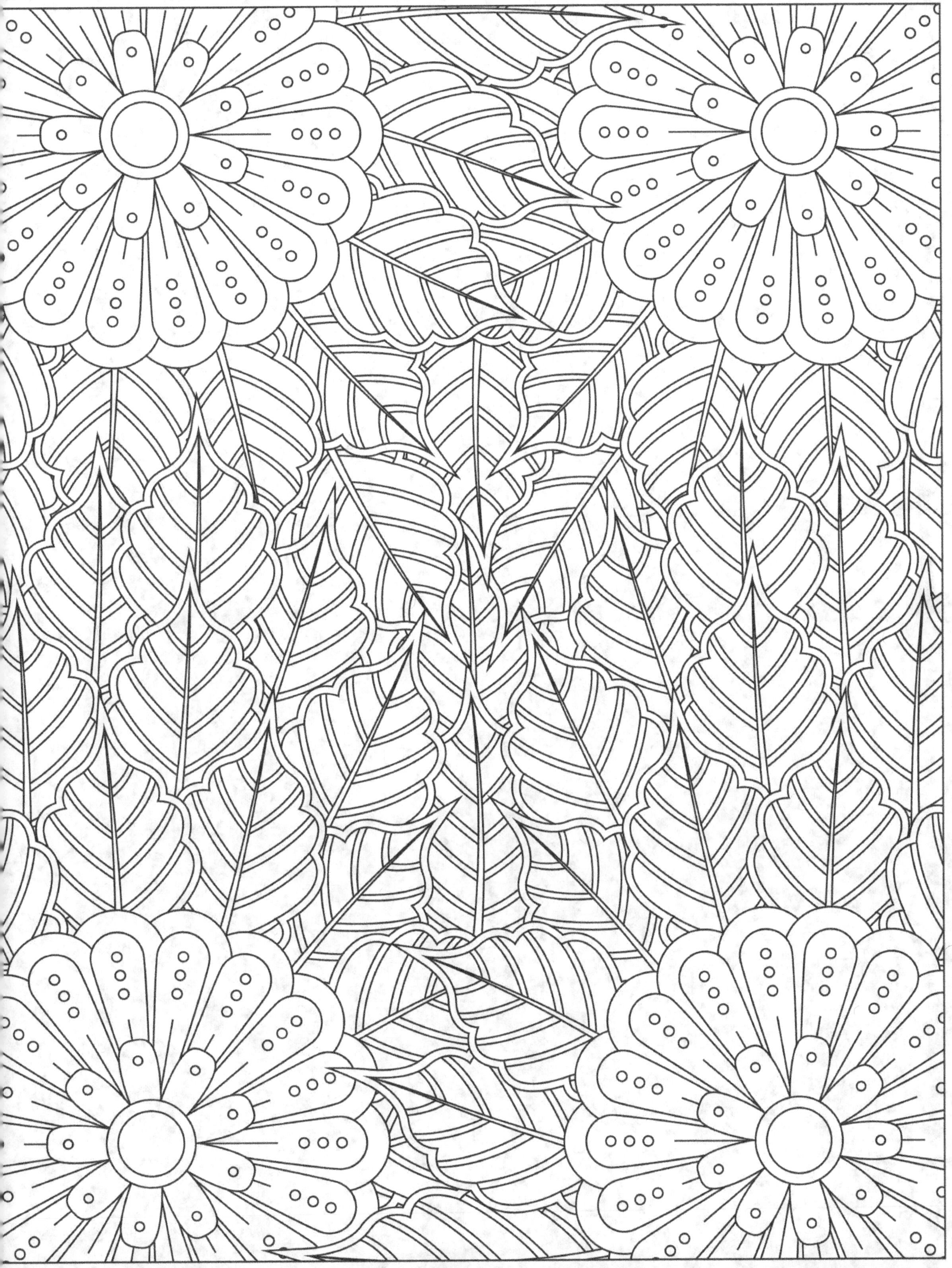

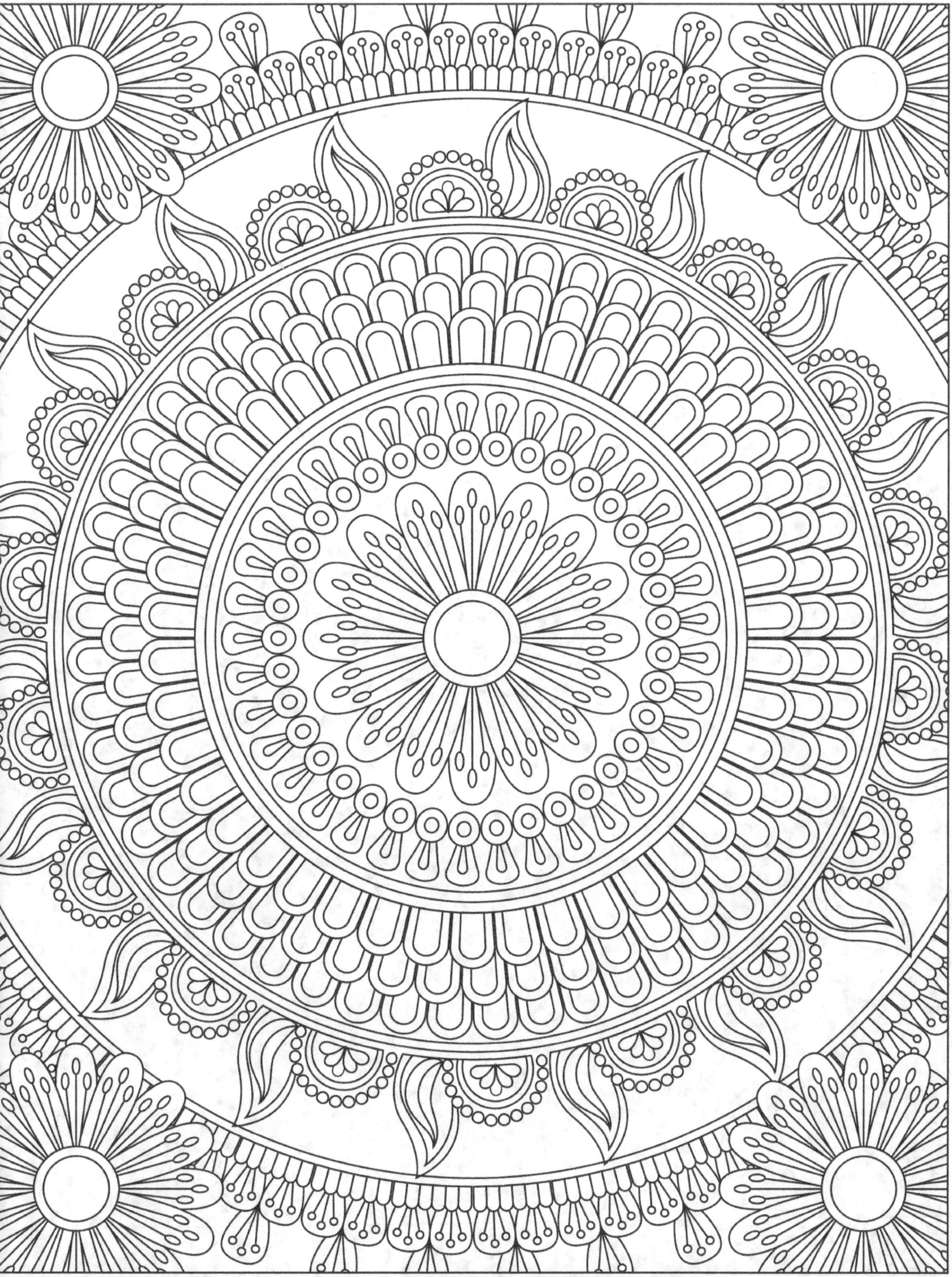

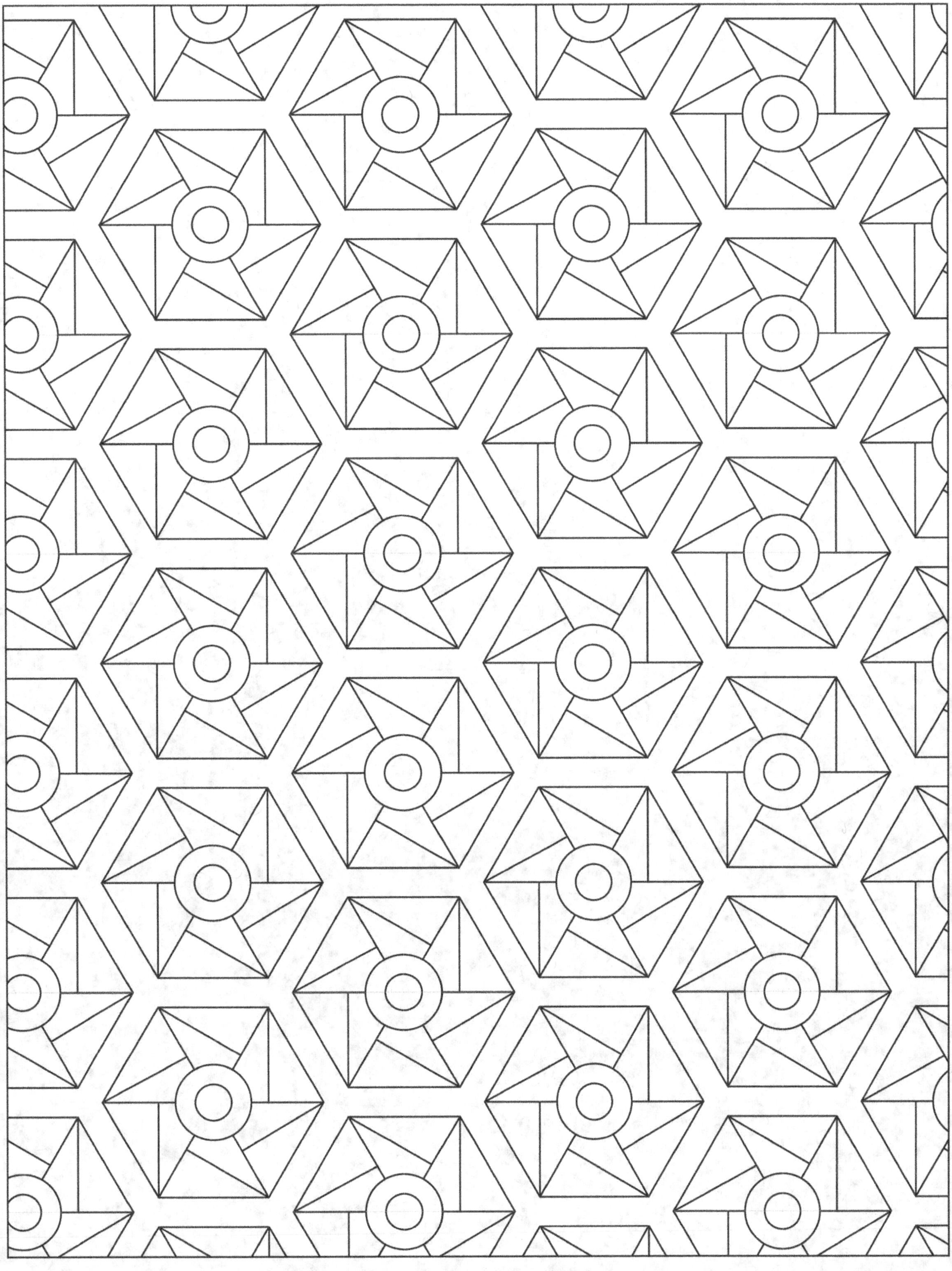

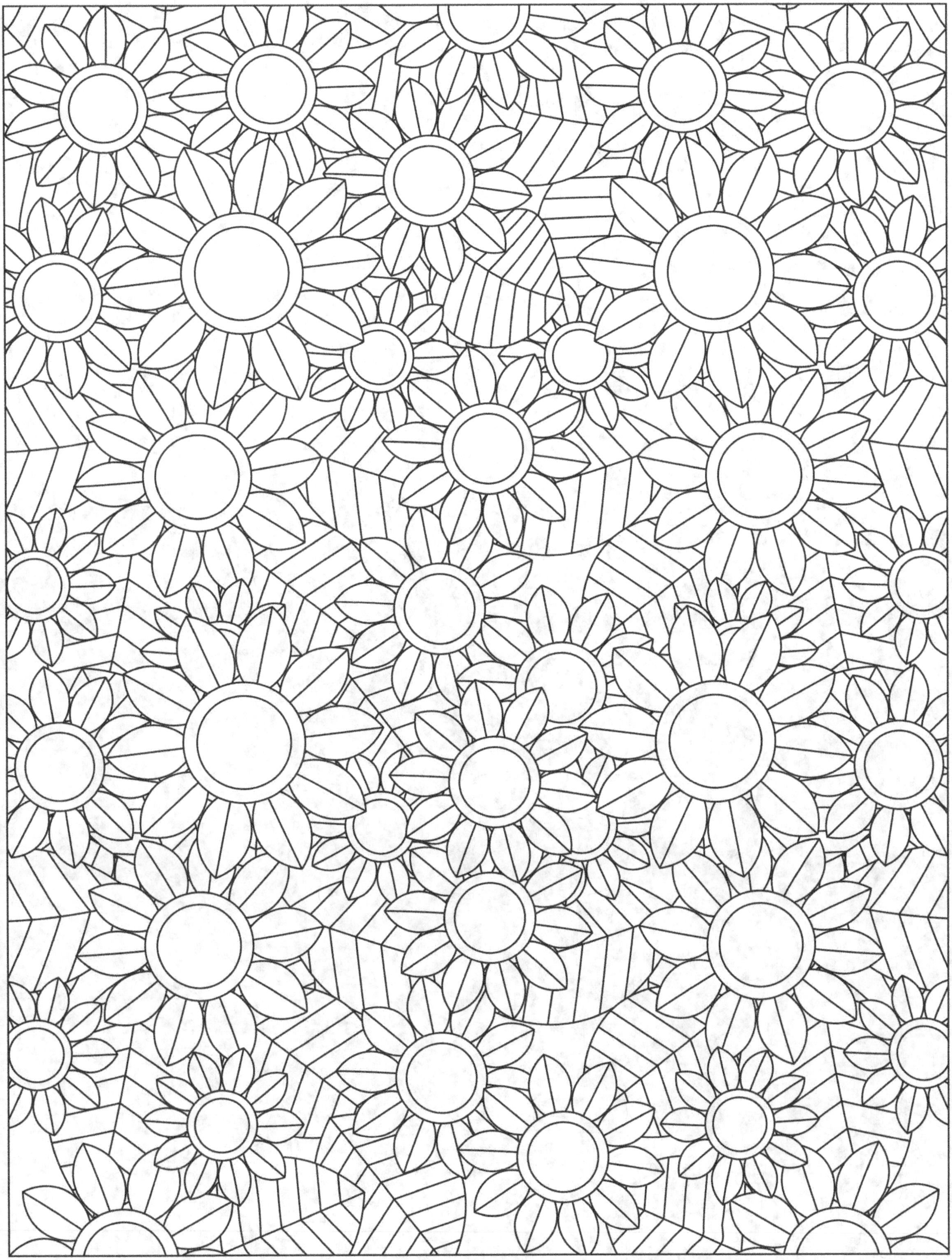

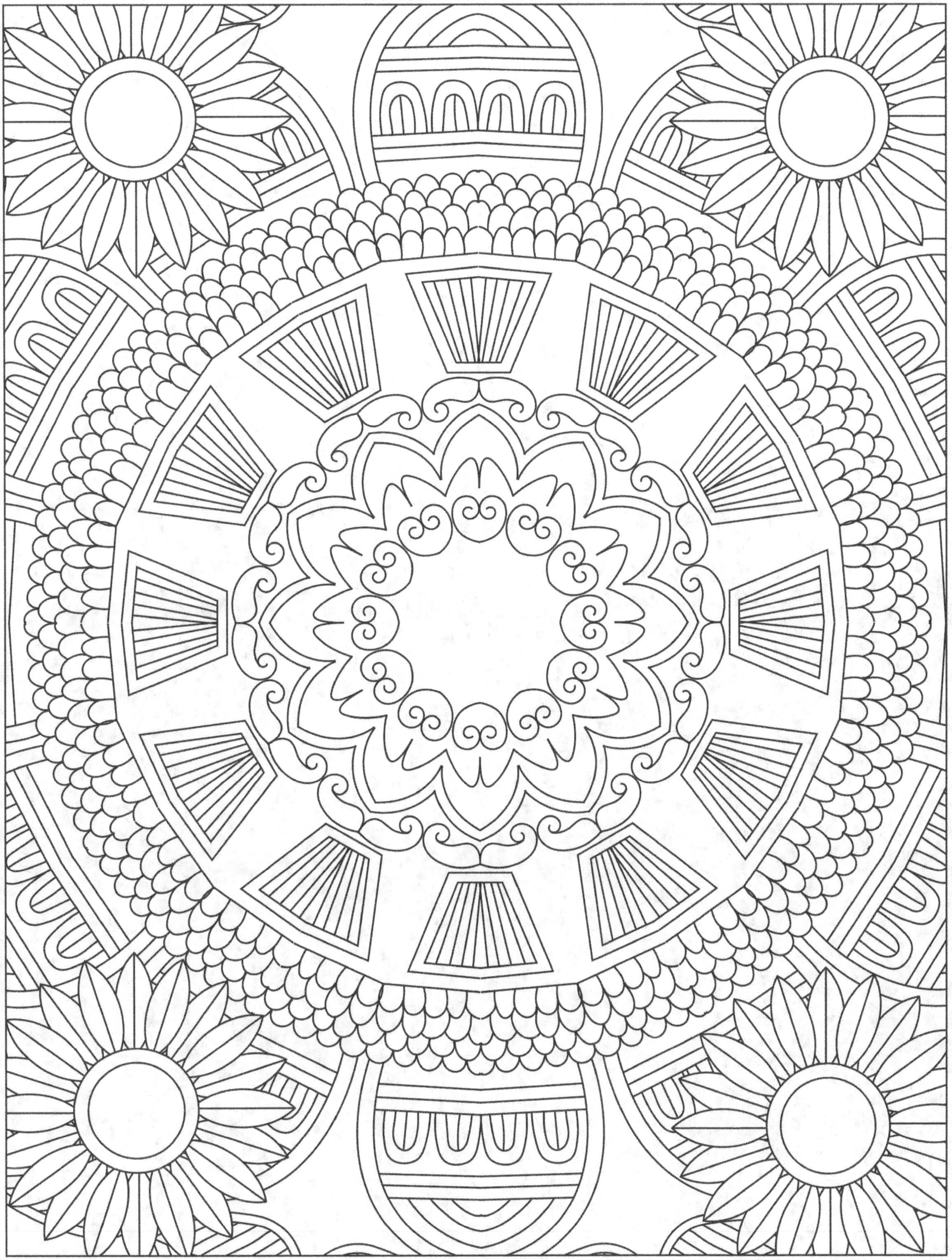

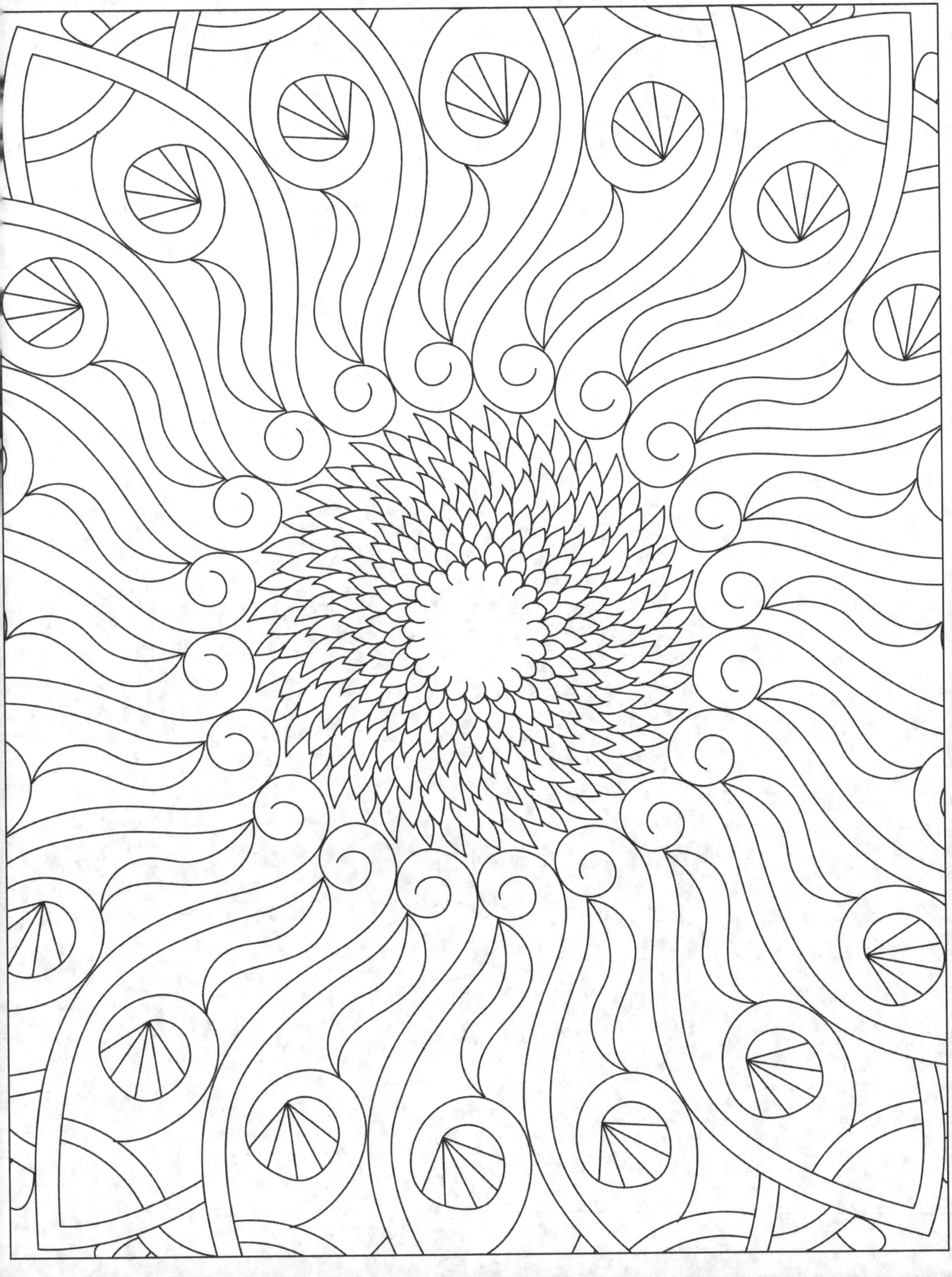

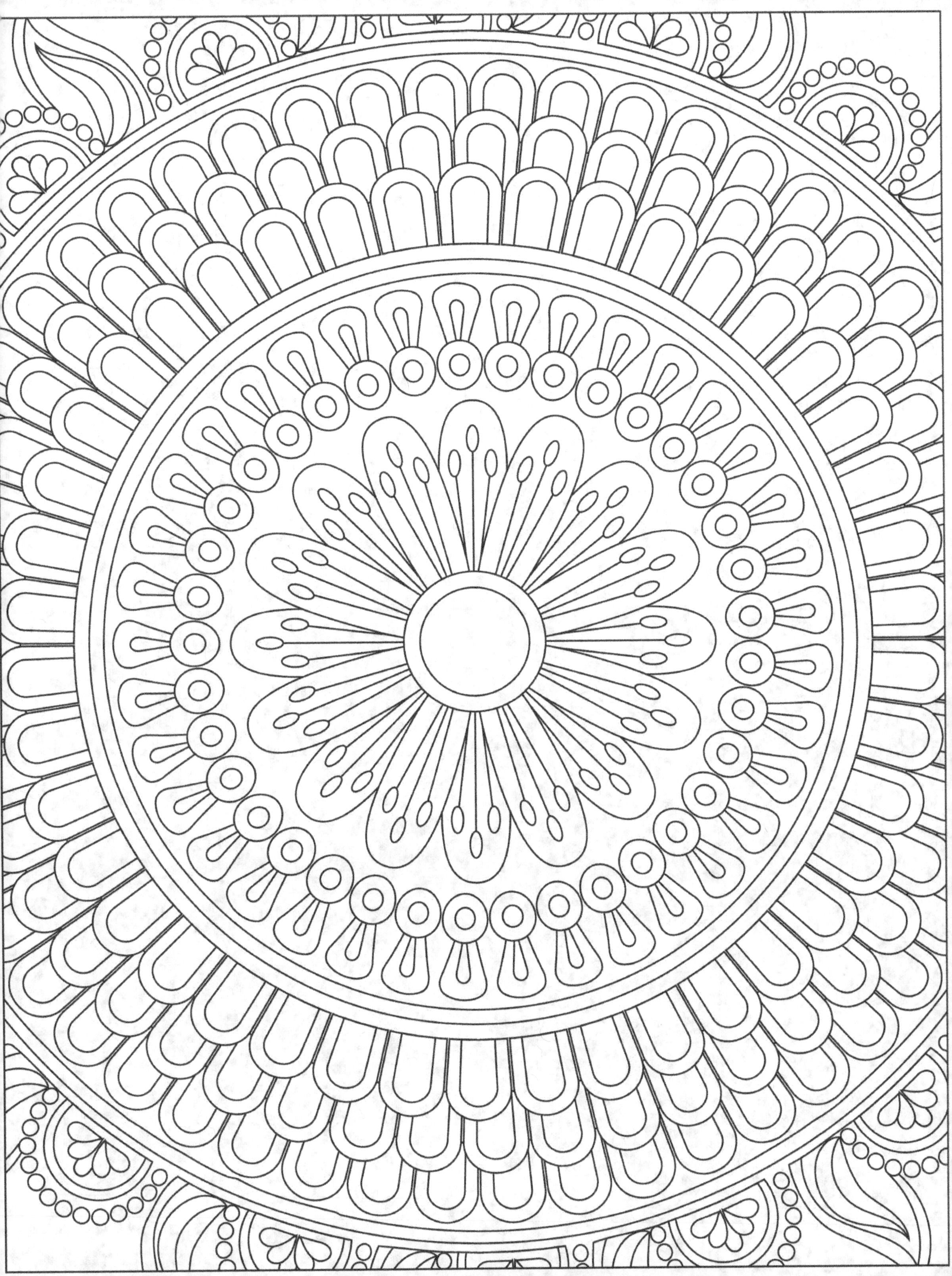

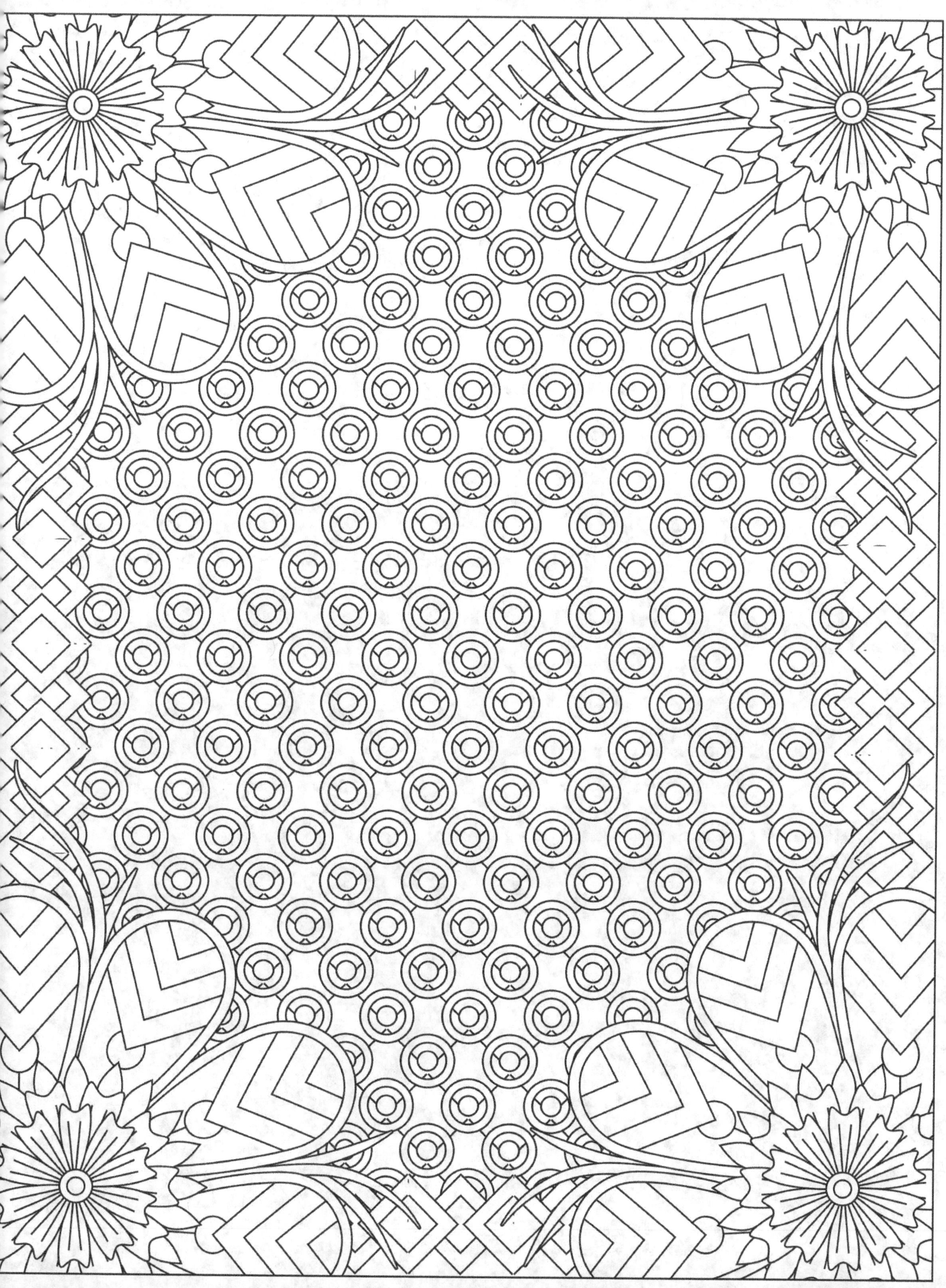

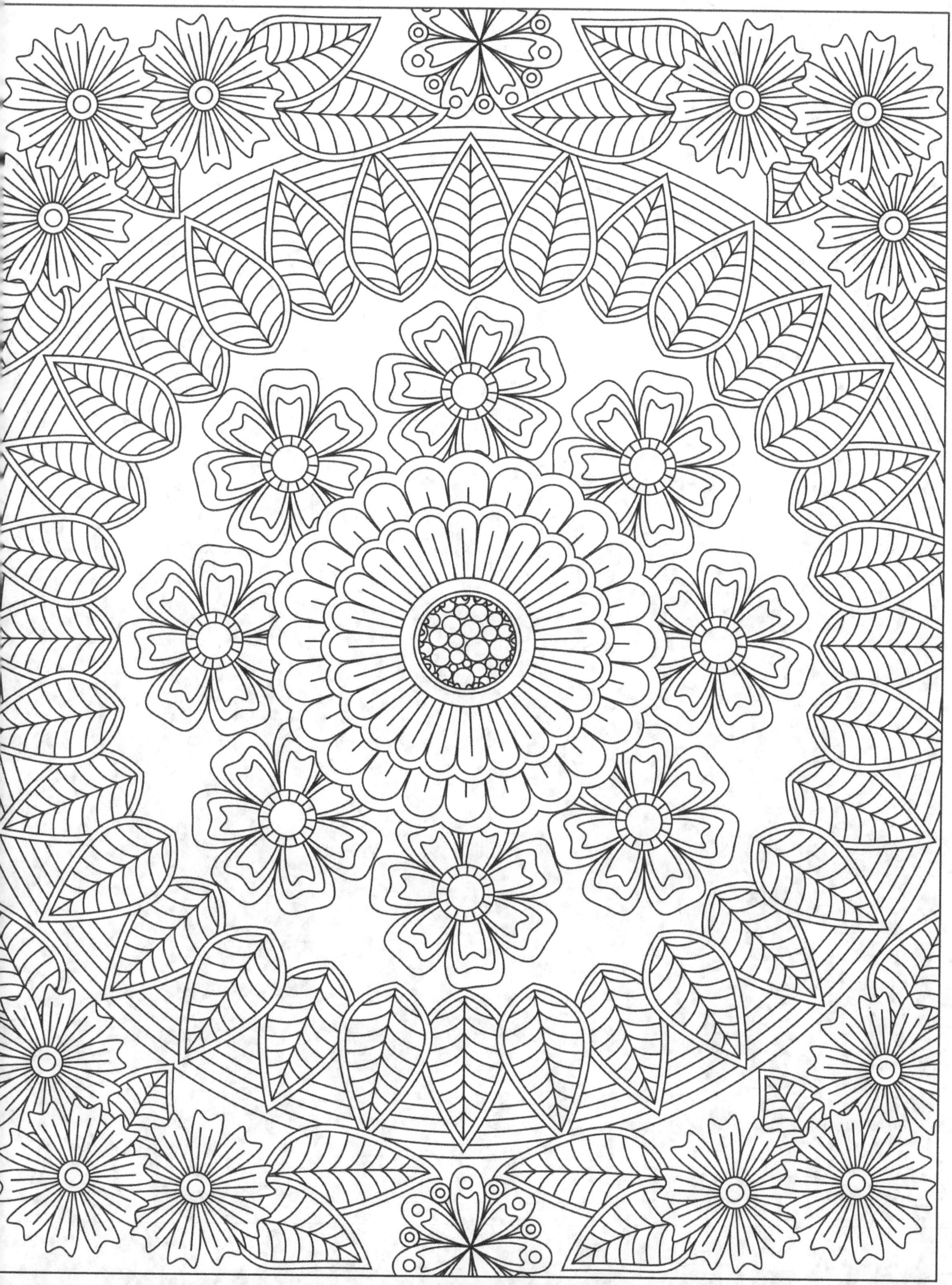

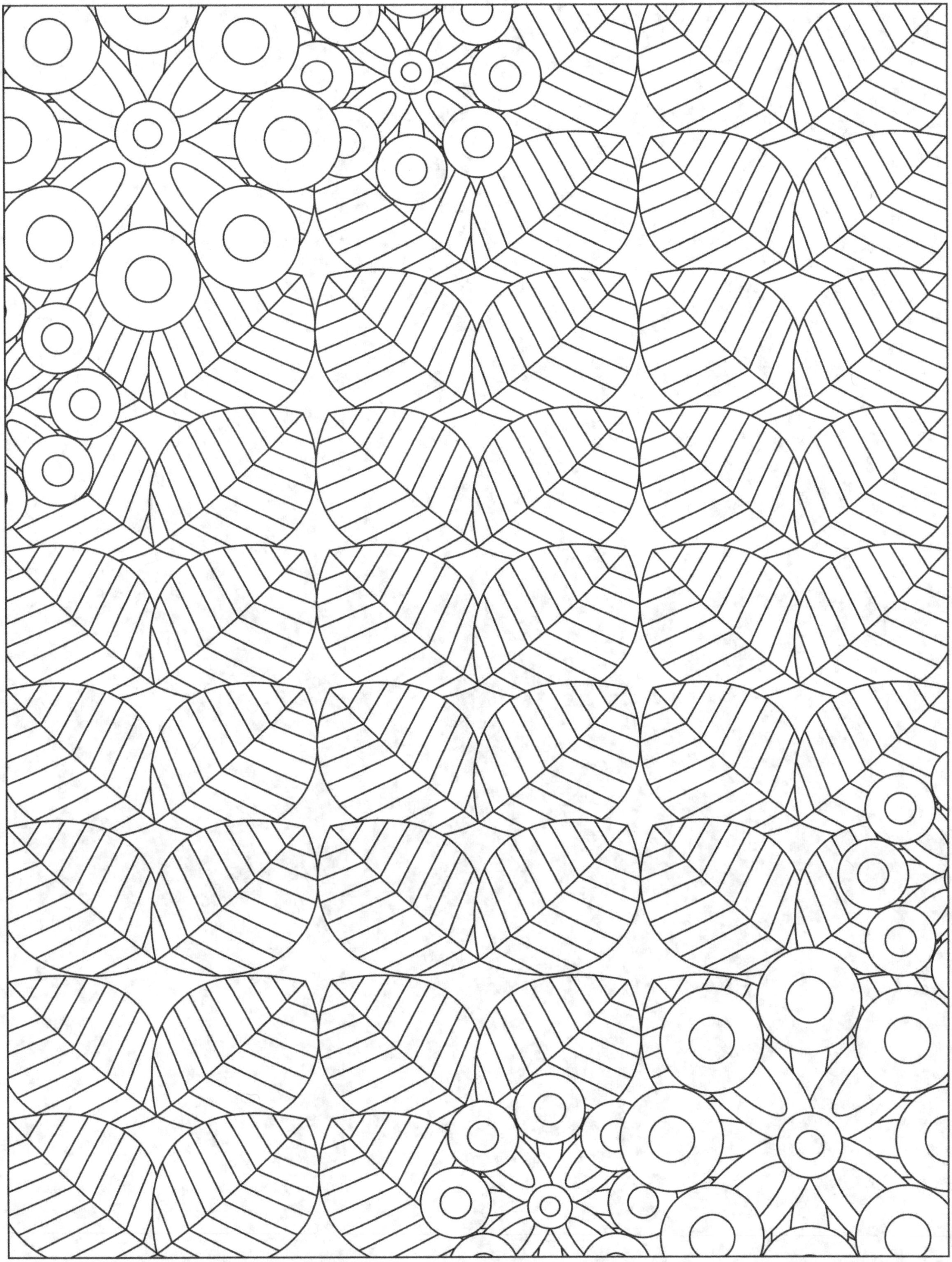

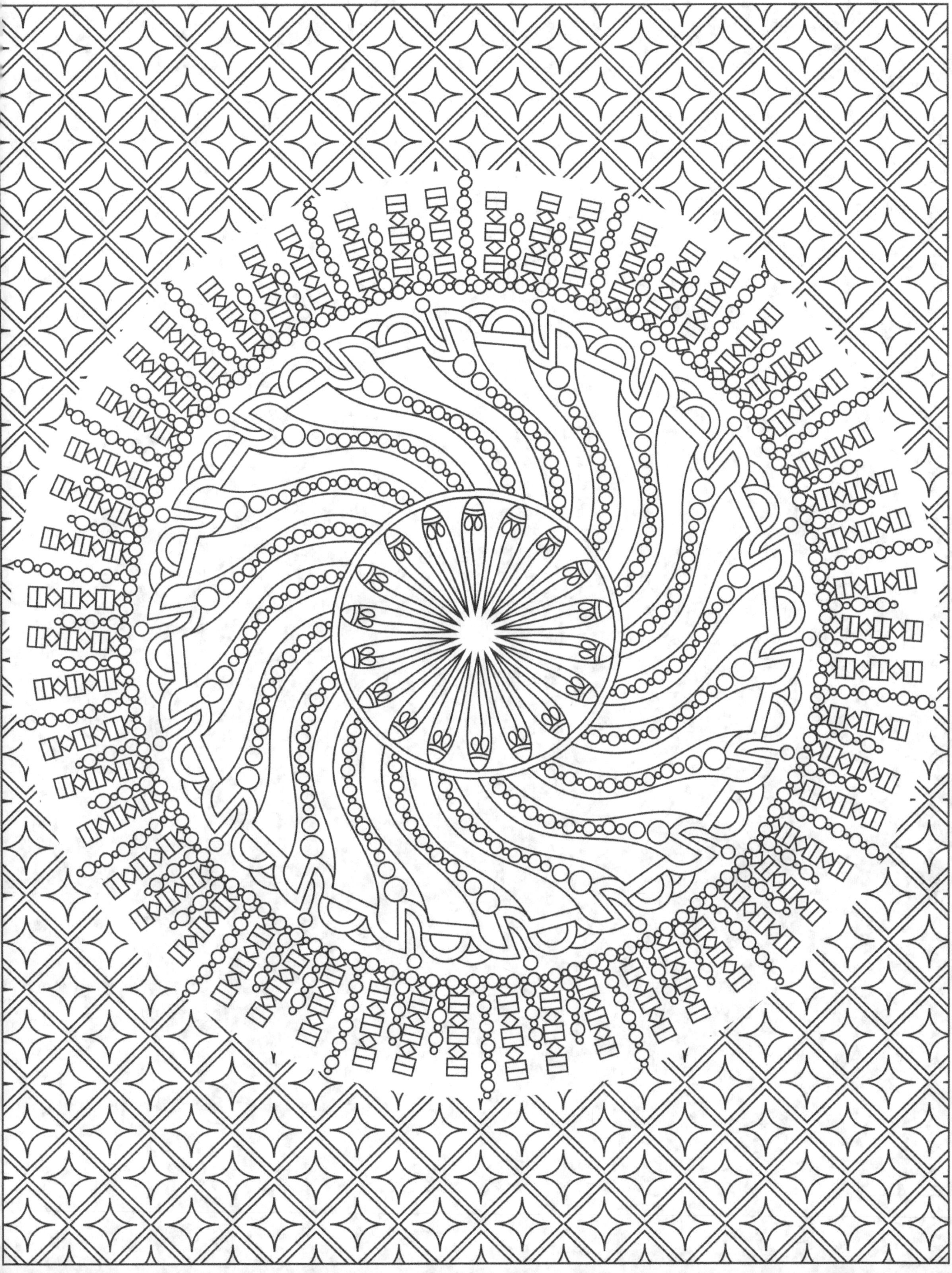

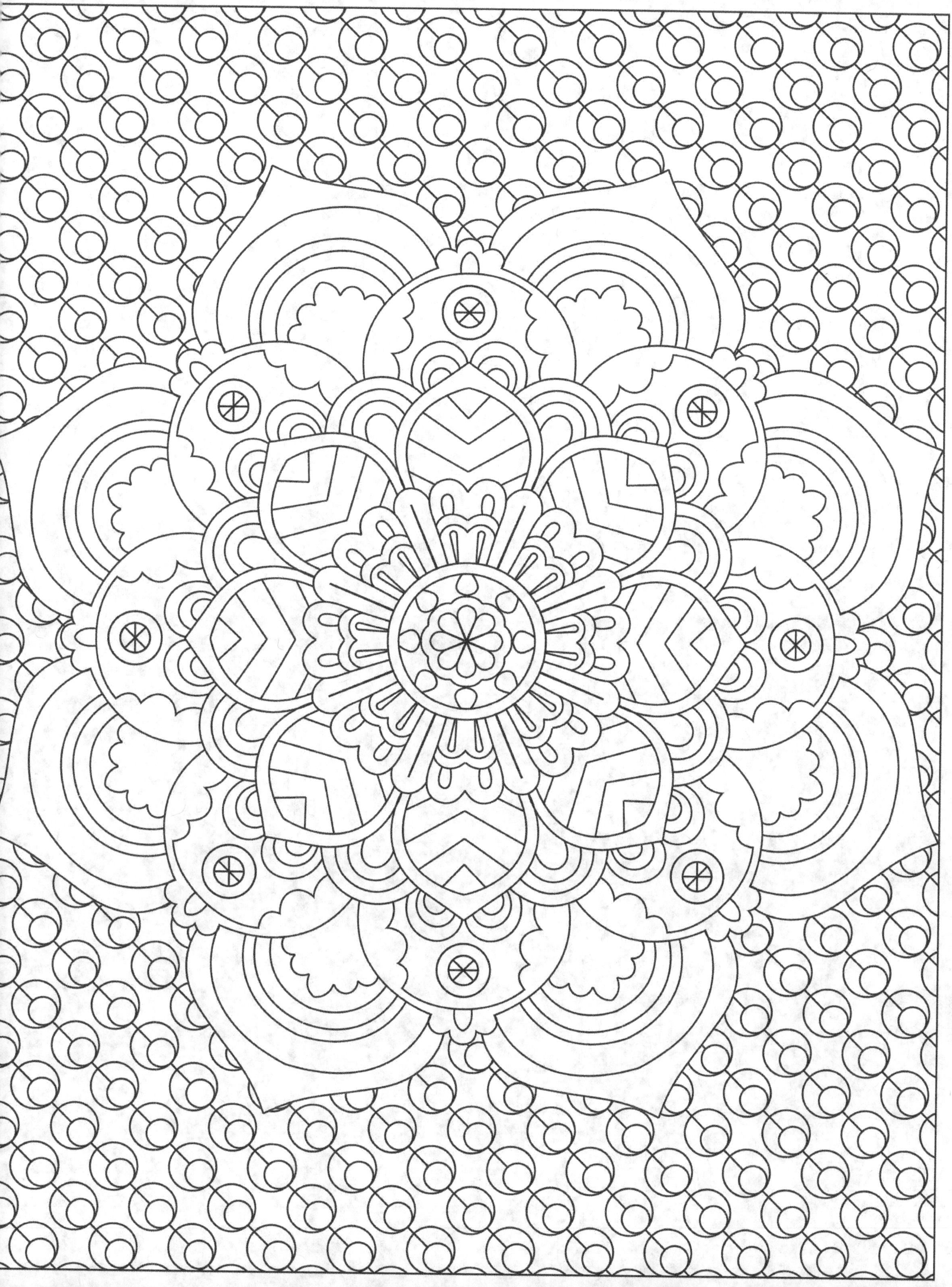

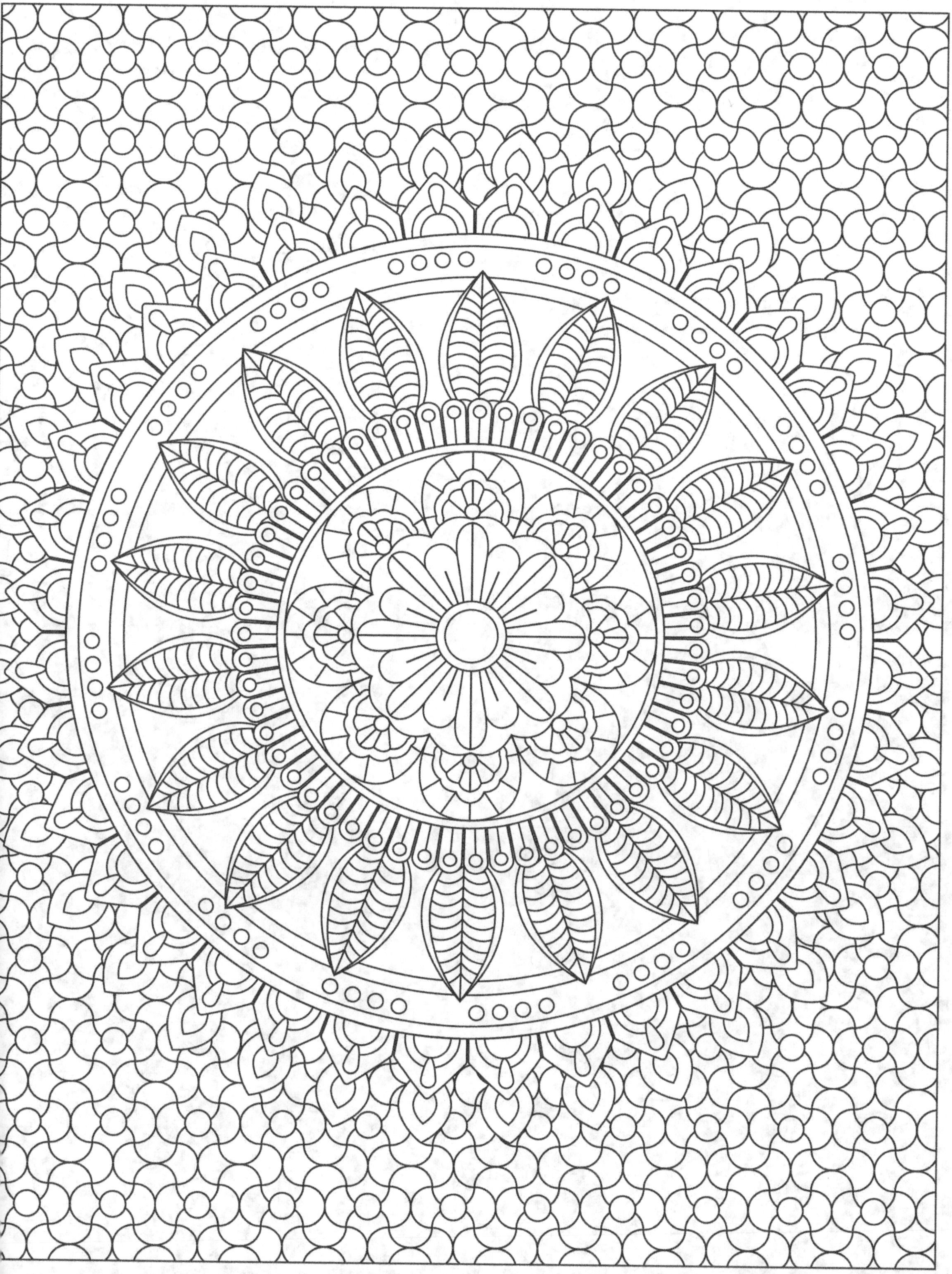

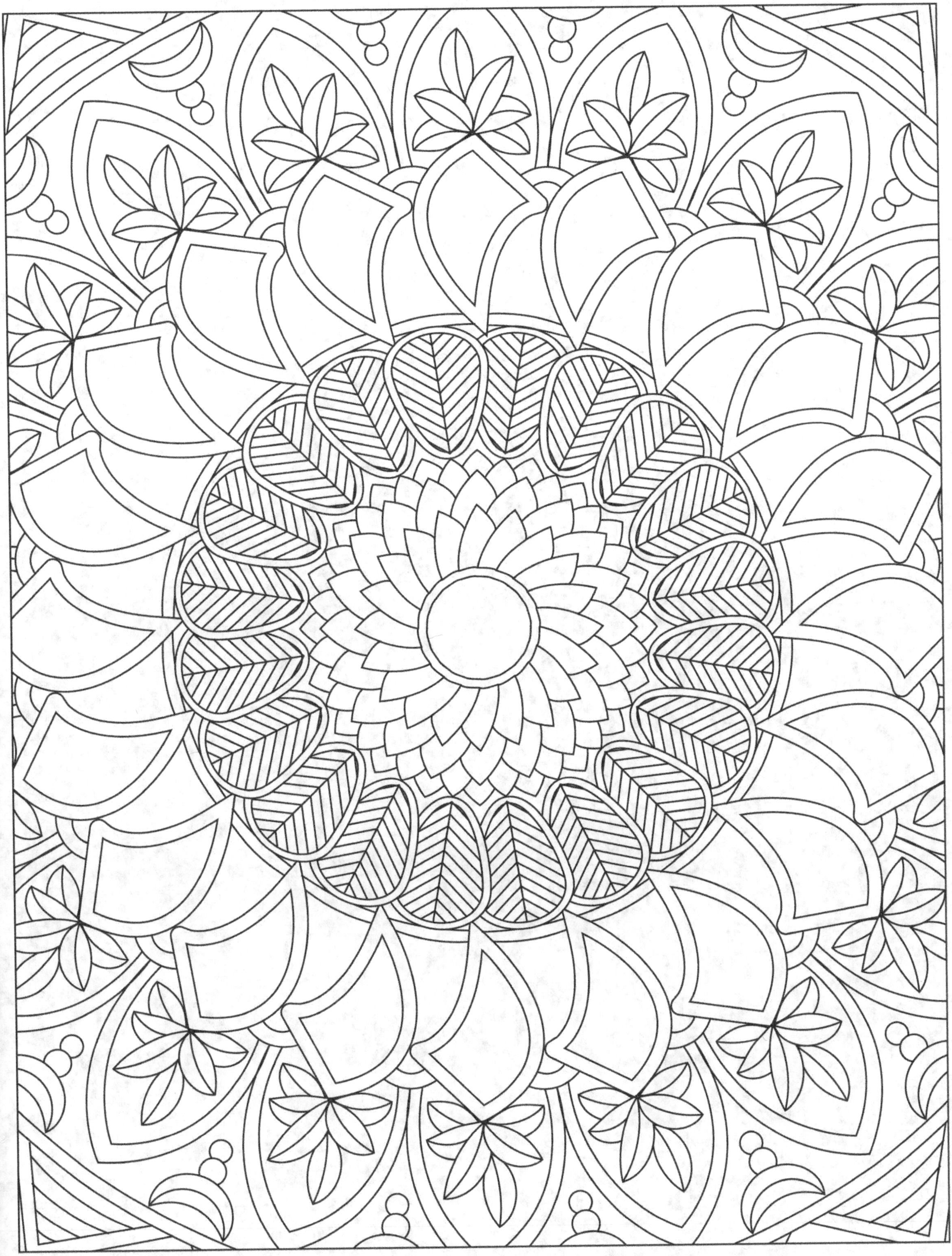

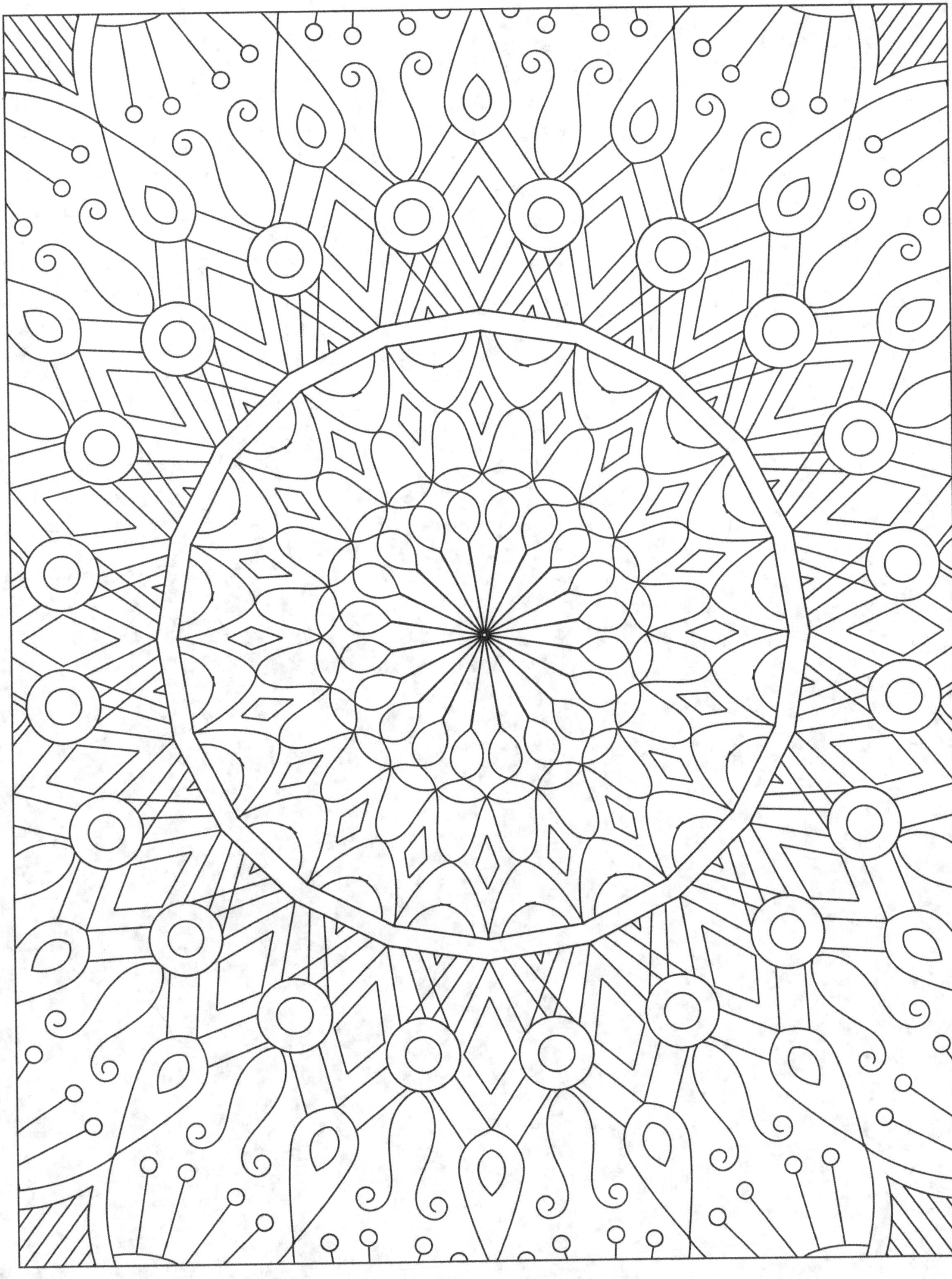

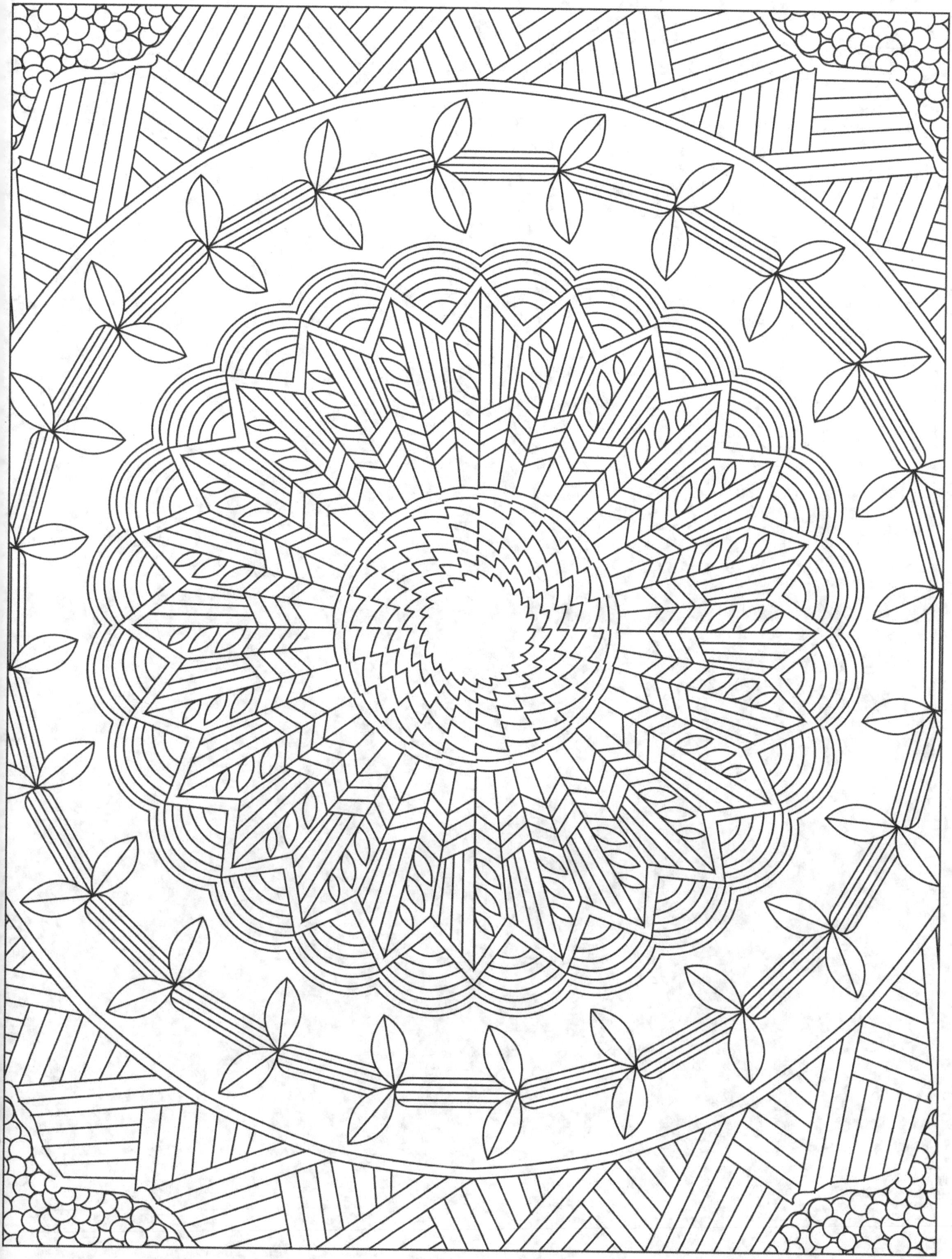

www.ingramcontent.com/pod-product-compliance
Lightning Source LLC
Chambersburg PA
CBHW082152230526
45467CB00044B/3041
* 9 7 9 8 3 8 5 5 4 3 6 4 9 *